WIND FROM ACROSS THE RIVER

A stunning new adventure of one man's fight against the Canadian wilderness.

Dan Nelson is a Canadian Indian, and he has just walked 350 miles across the Northern hills to find backing in Yellowknife for two gold seams he has found. He meets an Indian girl, Sam, a huge stray wolf-dog called Kayuk and a crooked dealer called Ziegel.

Dan returns home to Fort Norman to begin preparations for mining the gold, and encounters Ziegler's ruthless tactics for beating him to the mine, in the form of the hired thugs sent out from Yellowknife to halt his progress.

What follows is an extraordinary story of courage and determination. The character of the Canadian Indian is here revealed in all its raw intensity, while even the dog, Kayuk, plays a vital and brave part.

An unforgettable journey through the desolate and unforgiving Canadian wild lands.

By the same author

The Last Butterfly

Wind From Across The River

by

MICHAEL JACOT

McCLELLAND AND STEWART

Published in Canada by
McClelland and Stewart Limited
The Canadian Publishers
25 Hollinger Road
Toronto, Ontario
M4B 3G2

Canadian Cataloguing in Publication Data

Jacot, Michael, 1924–
Wind from across the river
ISBN 0–7710–4391–0
I. Title
PS8519.A44W56 1984 C813′.54 C83–099342–8
PR9199.3.J3W56 1984

Printed and bound in Great Britain

To Margaret

ONE

The young man stooped and drank from the pool beside the lake. The water was cool but it did not quench his thirst. Somehow his thirst was linked to the distance he had walked and to the desire which had driven him towards his goal.

Now it was almost in his hand. He had arrived. Up ahead there was a path through the massive granite slabs, worn marble-smooth through centuries by the mocassined feet of men as they made their way to the fishing grounds on Great Slave Lake. It was surrounded by poor, stunted Arctic pines and poplars clinging with finger-roots to an almost soil-less grasp on life. Above, a dozen or so of the great Yellowknife ravens swung out over the lake in search of prey. Beyond that was the town.

He turned to climb the steep hill towards it. It was a hot morning, a typical Arctic August morning. The sweat was already trickling from his collar, soaking the shirt under his pack. He sang quietly to himself. He was nearly there.

He could see over the brow now. More ravens, this time

salvaging among the garbage outside the cabins on the edge of town. He had done 350 miles, walking six days. He was tired but too excited to know it. He had come because he wanted something very much and the thought of it had consumed him during his journey.

He was known to be a very serious and purposeful young man who stuck to the traditions of his ancestors. He had lived almost his whole life in a small settlement on the mouth of the great Mackenzie River, where it rolls into the Beaufort Sea. This was the first time he had come to Yellowknife.

At the end of the month he would be 21, which in a white man's world meant he was a man. By the laws of the Cree he had been a man for six years already. He knew much. And he also knew little, which meant that he knew a little how to deal in white man's ways. He had been educated in those ways at high school and by his elder brother now studying in California at the university. But he had poor experience at putting them into practice. Now the time had come to do so. He was nervous, but he was confident.

He swung his broad, tough frame up the last few paces to the very edge of town, his amber, flat face, with the deep-set brown eyes, like polished mahogany under the sweat. He looked older than his years. His arms were big and hard, his legs long, swinging easily from the hip, his feet moving noiselessly. His nose, the rudder of his face, was long, thin and ending in a point, almost like a crow's feather.

The top of the rock at the old town in Yellowknife sloped down on all sides, being connected by a small causeway of a road which led to the modern ugly Canadian town—a mixture of ten-storey high-rises, distasteful government-designed housing and ramshackle hotels.

But all around the young man was the old town—a different sort of settlement, something like his own, only much bigger. There were cabins and shacks, some trim and clean, others decaying, surrounded with years of garbage and peopled with dog-shit. It was an ugliness, a homeliness filled with a character he knew. But in both towns the closeness of everything was oppressive. He wanted to run.

Over 10,000 people lived here. All his people in the huge lower Mackenzie River basin didn't add up to much more than half that figure.

He withdrew his eyes and refocused on something quite close. Not thirty feet away, standing against the side of a rough-hewn log café, was a girl. She was in her early twenties, he guessed, a *métis* and her hair done in a thick bun at the back, twisted tightly from her face so that her cheeks, reddened by the sun, were polished and stretched taut over the bones as if they were carved by an artist.

She wasn't looking at him. But she knew he was looking at her. He could tell. She was pretending to pat a dog. It was a giant animal, standing nearly three feet at the shoulder, with grey and brown matted hair. It carried its tail down, like a wolf. At first the young man thought it was a wolf, or at least mostly wolf. Perhaps some trapper had left its mother outside so that she would mate with the wolves. This produced much tougher pups, but the authorities forbade the practice for the animals could turn vicious.

The young man took a closer look at the girl. Her hands were large and long-fingered. She fondled the dog, rubbing its ears and stroking it under the chin. They were confident hands. Each stroke had strength in it.

He took a step across to her. Out of the corner of her eye, she noticed. Her mouth was generous, but now tightening at his approach.

"That dog yours?" he asked seeing the badly matted coat.

The dog was fully grown, yet with a lot of play in it. He sat on his haunches and pulled it towards him to make friends, feeling the muscles in its shoulders and the power in the thickness of the neck. The dog started to lick the sweat off his face. He pushed it away playfully, and, now his sudden friend, it made as if to attack, lying doggo on its stomach and then bounding happily towards him. The girl laughed. She was very pretty. He stood up.

"One hell of a dog you've got," he repeated.

"Never saw him before this morning, came in all messed up, and his paws bleeding from the rock. I fed him and he won't go away."

"Could use a good brush," he said.

The girl was at the door of the small café now, her arms across her chest and her legs crossed as she watched him with the dog.

"Where are you from?" she said.

She was aggressive in a pleasant way. Attractive too, but sort of tense, like an animal, her eyes darting.

"Fort Norman," he said, "I've just come up river."

"Fort Norman's the coldest place on earth," she said. "I was there two winters ago."

She shifted her hips, relaxing one and accentuating the other. She was smiling now, but still on her guard.

"It's the wind that makes it so cold," he said. "Blows across from the other side of the river. Comes right from the mountains."

He was looking at her now, but still stroking the dog for confidence. He smiled back, knowing that she was warming to him and liking him. "It was eighty below zero last January for ten days. The wind chill killed six people," he added.

"It was bad here too," she said, her mouth now relaxed.

He stood up and dried his hands on his jeans. "I hate the wind. More than anything I hate it. But Fort Norman is my home and I'll stay there when I settle."

They looked at each other for a second and broke into smiles again. "You look as if you could do with a cup of coffee," she said. "Come on in and I'll pour you one."

"Sure," he said, "I could use some breakfast too." He followed her inside the cabin and watched her go behind the bright arborite counter, while he slipped onto a stool. It was a small place, five or six tables, groceries, old-fashioned but very clean.

"My name's Samantha Cousins. Sam," she said, working the coffee machine.

"I'm Dan Nelson. If you've been to Fort Norman you'll have heard the name. There's plenty of Nelsons there."

The dog had followed him in and was lying with its nose on his left boot, pretending to be asleep. Dan experienced the weight of the animal for the first time.

"What do they call him?" he said.

"I've been calling him *Kayuk*," she said, now seemingly relaxed.

"Down river by my place, that's the name for a big brown dog," said Dan.

"That's it," she said. "Sugar?"

"Thanks. Hey there, you big brown dog!" he said rubbing its nose with his other boot.

There was a pause. The girl had her back to him while she heated up the grill. There was something about her that made Dan unsure of himself.

"Two eggs? Any bacon?" she said.

"Yes, bacon and two eggs. Thanks."

She turned to face him now, "You staying long in town, Dan?"

He felt himself blush under her gaze. The girl was even prettier once he got a closer look. She continued to glance back at him from time to time as she cooked.

"I've some business with Ted Ziegel."

"Oh, Ted. Ever met him?"

"No. First time in the big city!" he laughed nervously.

As she handed over the eggs and bacon he saw that her nose was long and thin, like his, but her eyes were deep violet.

She leaned on the counter as he started to eat. "When are you to see the big man, Ted Ziegel?" He detected a warning in her words.

"As soon as I've had my breakfast." He changed the subject quickly, purposefully. "Is this your place?"

"My mother had it. She died last winter. I came north again

to try my hand. I was out in Edmonton training to be a nurse when she died. I think I like it up here."

"Some people don't. My brother's in California at UCLA. He's going to teach. Every time he comes back he says it's the last time he'll come."

"Well, there's a lot out there. No doubt about it. It's the place to make money."

"I've never been out. I don't want to go," he said. "This is my land, my people. Yours too," he ventured.

She was looking out across the counter now, out through the window again, with that liquid look in her eyes. He chanced a long look at her. The dog shifted its head on his boot and snorted at something in its sleep. He knew what her eyes reminded him of now—rain against the sky in summer.

There was a peace in the air. After the food Dan felt his tongue loosening. Yet he knew he must guard it. He'd promised himself he'd tell no one. He paid the girl and she gave him the change without looking at him or saying another word.

Finally he said, "Well! Wish me good luck with Ted Ziegel."

"Oh yes! All the best."

"You turned off your motor or something?" he added.

She was embarrassed. "Sorry. A habit. My head gets full of useless junk. No offence." She was looking at him again now almost daringly, like when he'd first seen her. He looked down, pretending to count the change.

"Will you be back?" she said. "After your business? Before you leave?" She held out her hand

"Oh, sure," he looked up, and took her hand in his. "You'll see me again for sure. Maybe later today."

"I'll look forward to it then," she said.

Outside in the dirt road that led to the main street of the new town of Yellowknife, Dan turned to see the dog was following him. He tried to send it away. He shouted at it too. But it just kept stopping like a statue while he shouted. And then moving on behind him.

When he arrived at the front of Ziegel's office it was still around, pretending it was just a shadow in the alley that ran down beside the office.

He picked up a stone and threw it to frighten it. But it dodged and then stood like a statue again.

TWO

The girl watched the young man disappear into the distance, not wanting to take her eyes off him, and amused by the antics of the dog. She hoped he'd keep his promise to come back.

At the small mirror which backed the cans of groceries behind the counter she reached up under the bun of hair at the nape of her neck and pulled the band off it, letting it cascade over her shoulders. She wondered what the young man had thought of her? She was always nervous with strangers and over-compensated by coming on strong. But there was something about the young man that made her especially want him to like her. It was more than just what was written on his face. There was an honesty and a determination in him. Yet he was just a boy really. She'd noticed him blushing when she looked at him suddenly. She liked that. And she also liked the fact he had some place to go. She wondered why someone like him would be so keen to talk to a crook like Ted Ziegel? Maybe she should have warned him.

She took a look at herself again, "I expect he knew I'm a

métis," she said aloud, "and that's why he wouldn't tell me his business with Ziegel."

Some people looked down on the *métis* because they weren't of pure race. Once, at her aunt's in Toronto, a guy had mistaken her for Spanish and she'd been pleased. She hated herself afterwards. Especially since she knew she was attractive enough to stand on her own, *métis* or not. It was different here in Yellowknife. Most people knew her and took her for what she was. Like Rod Ziegel, Ted's son, with whom she'd gone to high school. The guy was a sweaty fat slob now, but he was a WASP and at high school he'd been in love with her. For God's sake! What was she thinking about Rod for? Rod was a nobody! He stayed around her too much. It seemed he was always there. Rod was a rich nobody!

The place was getting her down! She was beginning to think of nothing else but herself. Hour after hour in the café she would stand and stare out at the scenery.

Her mind flitted from thought to thought, wondering why she'd given up nursing, why she was despondent so often, why she was trying to lose herself in anything that seemed different or exciting. None of these thoughts ever took her anywhere. They were never completed. The trouble was that she knew there was something better around but she didn't know what it was. So she let her thoughts jump around the world of fantasy and expectation hoping that one day some great, unrealised dream would suddenly become reality.

Through her jolting thoughts there came a face. Grinning at her through the window. Rod Ziegel. And beside him his friend, Cunard, their noses pressed on the pane. Ziegel like the flat-headed Pole he was, and Cunard's thick Slavey features a caricature of an Indian tough guy.

"What's my goddam girl dreaming today?" It was Rod Ziegel.

"I'm not your goddam girl," she snapped.

"Coming to the party tonight?" he went on.

"Which party?"

"Me and Cunard are going over to Fatty's after supper. There's dancing and Gerry's bringing some grass he got from Mike Sargent. Most of the gang will be going. It's for Dorothy. She's leaving in the morning."

Cunard stirred the ice in his coke. He glanced shyly up at her. He was older than the guy who was just in but he seemed younger. She didn't like him anyway. He was an Indian yes-man.

"Well, you coming or not, Sam?" Rod said.

"Maybe I'll come. Maybe I won't. Probably not. No. I don't think I will. I don't want any more trouble."

The two men looked at each other.

"Suit yourself," shrugged Rod.

Last weekend Cunard had made another pass at her. He was egged on by Rod, she was sure. The guy never did anything without Rod's backing. Even when he got drunk and went wild.

No. If Cunard touched her tonight, it would be the last time.

Rod leaned over, playing the lover, "C'mon, baby, give us a kiss. You'll come tonight?"

She avoided his lips and left the decision in the air. He took a doughnut from under the glass and munched on it as he left.

When Rod was outside, Cunard stopped stirring his drink. He looked at her suddenly. He grinned sheepishly.

She said, "Go on. Go after your fat friend. I've got things to do."

Cunard said, "Pack of Rothman's, Sam," and he caught her arm as she handed them to him. "Maybe tonight," he said making sure Rod was out of earshot. "Maybe we can go for a walk or something?"

"Not on your life, baby." Sam couldn't stand the way he gripped her arm, and she jerked free. "Go on. Get out."

With his mouth still open and his eyes crinkled in a secret grin, he tore open the pack and pitched the wrapper on the floor.

Sam went around the counter and picked it up.

"I'll tell you what," she yelled, as they climbed into Rod's car, "I'll come to Fatty's and I'll bring a friend. I'll be there." The engine roared in reply. The car jolted over the rocky excuse for a road.

"Nelson? Dan Nelson. That's what he gave as his name." She repeated to herself, "Dan Nelson."

THREE

Ted Ziegel didn't scare Dan the way he had expected. But Dan never trusted him from the moment he saw him. It wasn't the blue pin-stripe suit, red and green tie and the gold cufflinks. What was untrustworthy was something not on the surface.

He told Dan to sit in a chair at the huge table he used as a desk. And then sat himself opposite, clicking his finger joints, a faint smile appearing at the corner of his mouth. Seeing him like that, nodding, rocking a little on the chair, occasionally using a forefinger to scratch his temple, you might say, "Could this man really be Ted Ziegel? *The* Ted Ziegel! The man most—people warned you against—surely not!"

Dan talked about Fort Norman, passing on useless gossip and waiting his time for the right moment to speak. Even though he wasn't scared he was nervous for he knew that somewhere underneath Ziegel's shell was a tough, unscrupulous man. Dan also had learned that when a white man like Ziegel looked like a friend, he either wanted something you had or he had decided not to give you what you were asking for.

Seven years ago Ted Ziegel had been a hard-rock gold-miner at the Giant Mine. One weekend, he and Lanny Harris had taken off across the Barren Lands, which stretch over a thousand flat, treeless miles across to James Bay, and near Coppermine had discovered something big. A sample of the ore they brought back was sent to Ottawa; it was so rich. It was thought they might be salting, which is enriching the sample with other gold to boost the worth of the find. But Ottawa confirmed the richness of the gold and they went out staking early that winter. It was before the time of the big boom in gold prices and there wasn't much of a rush. Gold was then selling for thirty-five dollars an ounce and not what it is today. But Ted Ziegel hung onto the claim.

He and Lanny Harris went out again the next break-up time and then Lanny got lost. It is easy for a man to do that in the Barrens, for one stone looks very much like another in the spring or summer and with the magnetic north being only a handful of miles away a compass can go screwy. But they found Lanny. Ted was on the search-party. The story hit the world's newspapers. There was an air of horror about it. Lanny had been found without a head. The inquest concluded some polar bear must have taken it. It sometimes happens in the Barrens in summer, when polar bears travel miles inland in search of salt and other nourishment to last the winter.

It was a very sad story and Ted Ziegel took care of Lanny's wife and kids with a handsome cheque. It was also a strange story, for if they had gone out in winter, even at sixty below with a seventy-mile-an-hour wind, Lanny might have lived.

A man can survive such conditions. Also on the Barrens the snow often carries a man's tracks for a long time so that they can be spotted by aircraft. And on top of that a compass doesn't act up as much in winter. No one quite understood why Lanny chose to go off alone in the Arctic summer like that. But Ted Ziegel was sure cut up about it and still had flowers put on Lanny's grave up by the Yellowknife airport and vowed that Lanny's kids would always be looked after.

When the price of gold rose, Ted Ziegel became a multi-millionaire almost overnight. He sold his claim to the Giant Mine for seventeen million dollars, and he registered the one Lanny was out looking for when he died and he sold that too.

Since then he had become known through North America, with an office in Toronto and a private plane. He built a new office in Yellowknife too and continued to work out of that place, because he claimed in the papers that he was a real northerner. These days he was becoming famous as a grub-staker, which is a man who gives supplies and food to Indians, Inuits and poor whites who go out looking for gold, silver, copper, uranium or any other material Wall Street fancies, and, if they find it, get a small percentage of the price of the original find, plus being fed.

If you are starving poor or plumb crazy, which most of them are, it's a good, lonely way to spend a summer or a winter. Sure beats trapline work and if you are clever you can often come back with a pelt or two worth a few hundred bucks. But Ted Ziegel did not grub-stake everyone. He was very choosy. He didn't trust too many people, and after the business about Lanny, people were not keen to work for him either. But some had to. He was one of the few real grub-stakers left. The search for Arctic oil and minerals had brought in the huge New York and Toronto companies with their electronic equipment and aircraft.

But there were still places, like crevasses in the rock, where the new tools couldn't or wouldn't work. And the men who were grub-staked by Ted Ziegel scraped at the hard rock and dug into the muddy soil to find such places.

But trust Ted Ziegel? There was a story going around that Lanny Harris had been dead for a week or more before the bear got his head, but no one could prove anything, and everyone saw how sadly it affected Ted Ziegel.

Looking into his eyes now, behind the patchwork of wrinkled skin, behind the opulent and overfed body, Dan could see steel. And behind the raw-beef neck, an undeviating purpose. Ted Ziegel was a man who would pay any price to get his own way. White men like this, Dan knew, often lost their fortunes in a crazy drive to prove their will strength.

"Well, Dan!" said Ziegel. "What's your business?"

"I want you to grub-stake me for three months."

Ted Ziegel puffed hard on his newly lit cigarette and sat back, his hands once again folded on his ample chest. He still held the strength and stamina of his twenty years at the rock face. His voice had a hard edge now.

"You are joking, young lad."

Nobody called Dan "lad" without his remembering it.

Ted Ziegel went on, "Why don't you ask your priest or someone who has access to money? Grub-stake! No. Sorry. I'm a busy man." He rose from the desk. Dan reached into his plaid shirt and produced a lump as large as his fist, wrapped in a rag which until recently had been his shirt. He undid it slowly, as a man should who wished to hold the attention of someone as greedy as Ted Ziegel. When he had finished there were four pieces of rock on the desk.

Dan put the rag underneath them, protecting them from the polluted cleanliness of Ziegel's desk. Dan ran his hands over the jagged rocks, feeling the places he had chipped the surface smooth for Ziegel's inspection, and sensing the shock of the revelation of his secret.

Dan then looked up at the motionless Ziegel. He saw the red-rimmed, lake-blue eyeballs roll slowly down in their hammocks. Dan detected no other movement, merely a quickening of breath.

Finally Ziegel took a step towards him. He was more clever than Dan had imagined.

"Who passed those off on you? What did you pay for them?"

The words sank into the silence. Then came back, expanding under the shock. Dan knew he must keep quiet. He prayed to every god he'd ever heard of—silence—golden, safe silence . . .

Eventually Ziegel said, "C'mon, Dan, who gave those rocks

to you? What sort of fool do you think I am? Have you come to me to try to get an assay?" Dan wasn't looking, and Ziegel was now behind him, above his shoulder. But Dan felt him move closer.

Dan said, "Mr Ziegel, I'll leave this one with you. You can get an assay done, if you wish. It is my own. I know where it comes from and I am ready to go and stake the claim. I need time, money and your co-operation."

Dan felt a hand slide over his shoulder and saw the powerful fingers slowly pick up the largest piece of rock. Dan's heart was beating so hard he was sure that Ziegel too could hear it. Dan turned on his chair. Ziegel had his spectacles on his forehead and a watchmaker's eyeglass in his left eye.

"Just suppose there's . . ." Ziegel began.

"No supposing, Mr Ziegel. It's the real thing."

Ziegel placed it back on the rag and walked to the window. From his stance, his hands behind his back and his weight on the balls of his feet, rocking back and forth, Dan knew he believed him and was thinking of a move to trap Dan into giving up as much as possible.

"I'll get an assay done for you."

"And the grub-staking?"

There was a pregnant pause.

"It's all out of your league, lad. Much better to cut yourself in with me and I'll have my son Rod and a couple of engineers get onto it—if—I say if—there's anything in it."

He came over and picked up another rock. He said, "Nahanni Valley, near the junction of the Laird?"

It was a silly trick. But Ziegel knew his gold. He wasn't too far wrong. Dan's face never flinched.

"The grub-staking?" he said.

A short laugh; "OK. I'll get Cathie in and dictate a letter to Manger at Fort Norman. That all right?"—a condescending pat on the back.

Manger was the local Hudson Bay manager and known for short-changing Dan's people. His was the only store in Fort

Norman and Dan had no alternative but to deal with him for his outfitting.

Dan stood up and faced Ted Ziegel. "And for the split, I want twenty per cent."

Dan saw Ziegel grow slowly purple.

"No deal. Forget the whole thing."

"I want twenty per cent."

"Highest I can operate on is seven. Look, I'm taking the risk. All you are doing is spending your time as you bloody well always do, wandering about and doing fuck all."

Dan held his breath, ignoring the remark.

"Twenty per cent."

"Ridiculous. Impossible. No, Dan. Sorry. You are a nice lad and a credit to your race, but I'm not a charity."

Dan stood up again and started to pick up his possessions.

"Look, Dan. I'll go a little higher but you may be on my payroll several months and it may all come to nothing—that's thousands I'm risking. Don't you understand?"

"Yes, Mr Ziegel." Inwardly Dan's heart was falling off a cliff, "I understand. Then I'll go *out* with the samples. Perhaps to Edmonton . . ."

At the door Ziegel caught Dan's arm.

"Tell you what. You are a nice lad. We'll draw up a document that if the assay comes back with high ratings . . ."

"What's a high rating, Mr Ziegel? You and I know that means nothing . . ."

"Say this assay is 0.666. Or even as low as .05 . . ."

"These are high ratings, Mr Ziegel?"

"OK, then I'll give you 15 per cent, but I'll take my expenses including the grub-staking off the top first?"

"Go call Cathie, Mr Ziegel."

Dan's heart was making music. He would have settled for ten.

Half an hour later he had a letter to Manger witnessed by Cathie. A letter of agreement between him and Ziegel and his remaining three samples in his hand and he stood at the door.

He wrapped them all in the rag that had been his shirt and stuffed them into his plaid shirt pocket.

"Better watch out what you do with those. Don't tell anyone about the deal we've got. You know enough for that, eh?" said Ziegel, lighting another cigarette and his eyes smiling behind the smoke. He held out his hand. Dan took it. Inwardly he too was smiling. He had Ziegel's money for his claim in the Mackenzie foothills and with that cash he'd have enough to stake his other claim in the next valley. And that would be his alone. It was big enough to make him a very rich man.

Dan nodded knowingly. Out on the street again the day was getting busy. It was nearly two o'clock, yet the sun was still high in the heavens. It would remain high until midnight at this time of year. The civil servants from the government buildings were making their snails' way back to their work. Indians and Inuits were making for the bars, already crowded with drunken commercial travellers, salesmen, clerks, prostitutes and bored wives looking for action. Taxis sped up the main drag, mostly driven by women. A line of station wagons, vans and private cars stopped at the lights outside Stern's pharmacy and Dan crossed the street. Yellowknife really was something else—he'd never have believed it.

When he got to the other side he realised the dog was still with him. "Kayuk," he yelled and the animal came up wagging its tail and itself like a piece of rubber band. He patted it and the two stood for a moment trying to make up their minds if they would visit the bar at the Yellowknife Inn or to walk up the street and take a look at the metropolis of the North, seat of government and commercial centre of an area twice the size of Europe, the Canadian Arctic.

The main street got the nod and Dan's eyes sparkled at the windows of the stores filled with appliances, lawn-mowers, grass-waterers, wedding dresses, women's underclothing and babywear. At the Criterion Theatre, across the street from the Bay department store, a movie with "exotic, irresistible sexplicit scenes" was showing. The stills outside looked tame enough. But Dan was getting hungry.

Later, the movie might be all right. It cost $8.50 to get in though. And that's just about what he had. At 6th Avenue, Dan turned and crossed, the dog still at his heels, heedless of the ravens which strutted the streets as if they owned the place. On the other side of 6th Avenue was a cheap-looking restaurant. On the window neon lights advertised "STEAKS". A menu was hung inside and the heat and moisture from the open kitchen misted over the window. A full dinner, $14.95. Fourteen-ninety-five for dinner! Dan's eyes went down the menu list. This must be some joint! Fish and chips were the cheapest. At $8.50—a bargain, complete with lettuce, slice of tomato and two pieces of toast. Where was he, New York, London, or Paris?

Up ahead a neon sign flashed on and off. "Girls, Girls, Girls . . ." Dan walked up, wondering how much they might cost. It didn't say, of course, but in the pictures outside one of them looked like Samantha's aunt or mother. Same sharp face, with a long nose and pretty decent figure.

Seeing the picture reminded Dan that Sam had a café. He hoped it was still open.

The walk downhill and up the small rocky slope to the old town was pleasant, moving from one world to another. In small neat cabins people were cooking supper. This was almost like home to him.

The screen door was open at Sam's and the place lit up with two kerosene lanterns, there being no running water or electricity in the old town.

Sam said, "Sure I'll get you supper. How was Ziegel?"

Dan nodded. "How much for supper? I've got eight bucks!"

"Tell you what, you go next door to Chuck Silver and get me a twelve-pack of Molson's and I'll cook you dinner free."

"How much is a twelve-pack?"

"Don't you know?" she said.

"I don't drink much," he confessed.

"Tell Silver you came from me. He owes me for two

month's groceries—bargain with him. Do your stuff, Indian man. Make the white man pay."

Dan slipped quietly and shyly out as he heard the frypan go on the oil stove. Minutes later he was back, six bucks shorter. Sam looked at him. "Not much of a bargainer, are you?"

"The guy's drunk," Dan said. "Just because he's white doesn't mean you can cheat him."

"Then I'll have to give you breakfast too, I suppose."

"I'm not staying over. I'm off home," he said, involuntarily clutching his hidden package.

"That's too bad. There's a party on tonight."

"Thanks. Got to make it back."

"Taking the dog?"

"Christ no! I've got five or six days' walk."

"How'd you like your steak?"

The question threw Dan. He'd never had steak. He said, "Oh, just do it how you like to do it best."

"Pan fried?"

"Yes," he said quietly.

"Where's the john?" he managed.

"Out the back. Loaded with flies. Take this." She handed him a can of mosquito repellent.

"Onions?"

Later, when he had finished the steak and Sam had spent a good fifteen minutes telling him what a real city like Edmonton was cracked up to be, he made to leave. Then she handed him a large slice of blueberry pie, and she broke open the case of beer.

"Want one?"

"Not yet," he said. "It's good pie."

"I'd tell you I made it myself, but the bread man thinks I'll fool around with him one day and he brings me pies. His wife makes them."

She took all the scrapings from his plates and added some old bread, throwing it out to the dog. She came back and took out a dish of water.

"Now how about a beer?"

"Well. OK," he said.

"Coming to that party, aren't you?"

"Nope."

"C'mon. I might need protection." She laughed and leaned further over the counter. He could see almost to her nipples down the front of her blouse. He blushed again. What was it about this girl that made him feel so young and insecure?

"C'mon and then you can leave refreshed in the morning!"

What if it is a trap? What if she is trying to get me to say I'm grub-staked? Maybe she's even working for Ted Ziegel? He brushed away these thoughts. She was smiling at him across the counter, her eyes on him enquiringly, as innocently as the dog.

"You come to the party and I'll give you food to take on your journey," she said.

"All right," he said, "I'll come."

After they'd had another beer she went round the back to the shit-house. Meanwhile he went round the other side of the cabin and found a soft piece of earth that had once been a flower-bed. In the shade of an overgrown bush, he dug a small hole and buried his papers and the remaining gold samples all inside the old shirt. He put a stone on top.

When he got to the screen door again the mosquitoes were out in hordes. "Come along," she said. "The party's only over the hill. Let's finish another beer and stroll over when we are ready."

FOUR

As soon as Dan Nelson left his office, Ziegel got on the phone. The only person he could trust was someone completely dependent on him, a slave figure, someone too frightened to rebel. This was his son.

Rod Ziegel had gone back to the house after he had left Sam's café. He had dropped Cunard off by the water, where the Indian lived on the edge of the old town, and now the little red Honda, his father's present for his last birthday, stood in the driveway of the pseudo-suburban dwelling that Ziegel called home.

Rod was now 25, overweight, slightly balding and carrying a thin characterless moustache. He had been born in the North and grown into one of those whites who are uncomfortable outside it. The dirt, flies, dogshit, tavern brawls and unregulated life suited him. He got along with people like Cunard, because they demanded nothing of him, and he was too lazy to give more than was absolutely necessary. He played, like a perpetual boy, snivelling when he didn't get his own way, and boasting when he did.

He was a big man, bigger than his father, and the teenage round of self-centred pleasure had yet to leave him, although he had yet to have his first sexual experience with a woman, only boasting of it freely and frequently. In a boyish way he preferred the company of Cunard to that of most girls, despite his local image. Whenever he got to the point of having to follow through on his boasts an impotent streak hit him and he made some excuse.

All that is not to say that he was a weak man. He had inherited the steel strength of his father, and like many men in his position he could even turn his weakness into a bitter determination that was without moral or logical grounds. Just as his father would risk his fortune to save his own dignity, so Rod could throw himself into a project without reserve.

When his father came into his money, people stopped saying anything, realising that Rod would remain a perpetual mischievous playboy, an obese Peter Pan whom they would have to suffer until the father died or the boy grew tired and left town.

One thing was for sure, the father still held the whip and even this afternoon, ten minutes after his call, Rod was in his father's office, seated in the chair recently vacated by Dan Nelson and listening with genuine enthusiasm to his father's enthusiastic story.

"You'll need to get somebody in—to help tonight," said his father.

"Andy Manowski will do it," said Rod.

Twenty minutes later, he called in at the Mermaid Café and picked up Cunard to whom he imparted a sketch of Dan's news. Together they climbed into the red car and made for the old town. Two houses over from Cunard's cabin they parked under the shelter of an unpainted frame building, once the end of a Hudson's Bay trading post and now falling into decay. Andy Manowski was their man.

FIVE

Andy Manowski had been trained as a butcher in Poland, and although his age was undetermined, he claimed he didn't remember the Second World War. He certainly looked old enough to have taken part in it. He had come to Yellowknife soon after the war and, like most immigrants, he had worked in the mines. He was a very powerful man with a heavy rock-like face covered with pale folds of thick loose skin which hung around his eyes and mouth.

He no longer worked in the mines. There had been an accident. Two of his fellow workers had been killed after an argument. One was Charlie Pierce, a young Slavey from Fort Smith with only a year's service at the Giant Mine, the other was Andy's brother, Tadeus. How it all came about was a mystery, but Andy had been laid off. The other men said he began to act strange down the mine, singing guttural songs, cursing and shouting to himself. That was twenty years ago. Since that time Andy had done odd jobs with a maniacal efficiency and total lack of human understanding. He could be hired to do anything, quietly and without feeling.

He spent much time alone, from his own wish as much as from the reluctance of others to be with him. He set traps, European fashion, among the grasslands along the banks of Great Slave Lake, to catch Arctic hares. Some of these he sold. He had an elaborate set of butcher's knives which he brought with him from Poland, and cutting up the animals was a ritual for him.

Andy lived in the abandoned Hudson's Bay storage hut in the old town, down among the rocky lakeside. On this day he was spending the early evening at the butcher's bench he had made outside the cabin. The gulls waited on the rocks around him for titbits which he flung with meticulous precision into the bay.

Cunard, who had been sent by Rod Ziegel to find Andy, sat on the brow of the hill above and also waited. He had eighty bucks in his pockets.

When he made up his mind what he was going to ask, Cunard rehearsed it a dozen times. Rod was sure to ask him what he'd said and then he started down the twisted path.

Andy never looked up from his work. The only acknowledgment he gave Cunard was in the extra delicacy he began to administer to the hare being skinned with his knife. He was like an animal showing off before its master, or a master carpenter making special of ordinary work to please onlookers.

Cunard said, "I got some work for you, Andy."

"It'll cost you," Andy said, sniffing the hare. He sniffed it all over as if he were a dog about to eat it, breathing hard and with his eyes half closed.

"It's for Rod, not me. I got cash."

The ritual over, Andy tossed the parts of the hare into a bucket of water and came towards Cunard.

Cunard was not a brave man.

"What is it you want me doing?" said Andy as he advanced, the bucket dangling from his left hand.

"This is Rod's job, understand. I'm his messenger . . ."

"Come to the fuckin' point, Indian," Andy said, putting down the bucket and picking up a live hare which he had attached to the cabin by a string.

Cunard started to explain and meanwhile the big Pole just stood blinking at him as if he didn't really quite understand. It took Cunard quite a lot longer than he had anticipated because he found himself having to go into details which he could never tell Rod he'd revealed.

"How can I tell which one? It'll be dark?"

"I'll point him out to you," said Cunard, "because Rod 'n' I will be there tonight."

Andy wiped his bloody hand across his mouth.

"How much cash'd Rod give yer?"

"Thirty bucks."

Andy took a step nearer.

Cunard held firm in his tracks.

"C'mon. He give yer more'n that," said Andy, "I reckon you got sixty at least."

Cunard wasn't ready to bargain too long. It was late and Rod was waiting in his car to go to the party. That night Andy Manowski was bought for fifty bucks.

He took the cash, and pocketed it. Then he hit the hare across the neck with the heel of his right palm and watched it give three kicks and die.

He never said he would do the job. He never even said he would be near enough to be called to do it. He went back to applying his skilful hands to the butchering of the newly dead hare.

Rod was sitting in the red Honda which his father had given him when Cunard ambled up.

"What did you tell him?"

"Like you said. Not to go all the way tonight."

"You stressed that?" said Rod. "Did he say he'll do it?"

"All settled."

'How much did it cost?" said Rod.

"Forty bucks," said Cunard thinking he was boasting of his

ability to bargain.

"Let's take the rest and buy some liquor."

The car sped back onto the road and Cunard cursed himself for exercising his inferiority complex. It'd cost him his own ten bucks.

"I hope that big prick from Fort Norman gets scared shitless," said Rod. "I just saw him fooling around with Sam and some beers." He smiled angrily. "And guess what? I think they're on their way together to Fatty's."

SIX

When Dan and Sam arrived at Fatty's place, they had drunk quite a lot of beer and Dan's head was light. He'd rarely been drunk before but he noticed that the drink did little more than make Sam less talkative. She fell into more long pauses during which she seemed unaware of his presence. In fact she had said nothing all the way up from her café to the screen door of Fatty's, which he now held open.

Fatty's was the old Esso warehouse on the land end of the dock, not far from Andy's cabin. It was a sturdy enough building with a tin roof and concrete block walls. It was cool and damp, with more than a twist of the scent of diesel fuel which it had once stored. Someone on the council or some such body had acquired it from the company and turned it into a sort of recreation centre for young people. Why it was called Fatty's no one remembered.

The place was fitted with old furniture, including a few reclining settees which had been dumped there as each set of the almost permanently transient population of the old town moved on to God-knows-where.

Tonight it was lit by two hurricane-lamps and was insufferably hot. Little sunlight got through the three small windows and the place was filled with the burdening noise of the voices of the people who seemed to have stuffed themselves into every available space. At first, coming from the evening sunlight, it was hard for Dan to pick out faces. Sam clung to his arm and she felt his neck muscles harden. She wondered why he was so nervous. He had been to gatherings like this before, but they made him shy and embarrassed. And with Sam clinging on to his arm, everyone seemed to be looking at them.

Some people were dancing and he was scared that Sam was going to ask him. He was a poor man on the floor.

"Don't be so uptight," Sam said. "Relax. Come and meet some friends."

She introduced him to a tall, fair girl who told him her name was Dorothy and that he must excuse her because she'd already had a lot to drink. Dorothy seemed even prettier than Sam, although Sam was a very pretty girl. Dorothy had a flat round face with an upturned nose and very light-blue eyes.

She said, "I heard all about you from Cathy, Ted Ziegel's secretary."

That statement made Dan more nervous. He rubbed his palms on his pants.

Sam said, "It's Dorothy's party."

"Yes. I work for the government," said Dorothy, and she giggled. "You'll find a lot of government people here," as if that explained why it was her party.

Dan took a last swig from his beer and put the bottle into a cardboard box standing against the wall.

"I'm going to get us two more beers," said Sam, and she left Dan standing beside Dorothy. He wanted to be out of this place and on his way. The closeness of the people and the atmosphere made him uneasy, claustrophobic.

When Sam came back with the beers, he said, "Let's get out of here."

"Come and have a dance?" It was Dorothy. "I'm going *out* tomorrow. I'm going to be married."

"Take him, Dorothy. I'll be over with Rod."

Dan, who had never yet met Rod Ziegel or Cunard, caught the look Rod was giving Sam. He wondered if there was something between them.

At last the slow, wailing beat of the old Hank Snow song, "You'll be my Buddy 'til the Sunset", came to an end and someone put on another disc and Anne Murray's voice blared at Dan above the heat and smoke, "Somebody's waiting, somebody's waiting, somebody's waiting here for you."

"What's up?" said Dorothy. "You just aren't in the mood?"

The sweat was hot under his chin and the palms of his hands wouldn't stay dry. He felt he should apologise and get out of the place.

A big fat woman in her late thirties, the flesh swinging over her hips in rhythmic bounces and her breasts like melons, was twirling on the centre of the floor in a mocassined square dance to Anne Murray's gospel beat. God knows who her partner was. Maybe she didn't have one. Behind her was an older man, with hooded eyes and a crumpled face, who strummed on a guitar, a tune of his own making, certainly not one of Anne Murray's making. Four or five younger couples were now on the floor. And in the corner two guys had pulled the mattress off a small bed and were lying on it smoking pot. Sam came over with another beer.

"Sam, I gotta leave," he said.

"He's not feeling so good," said Dorothy impulsively. "I agree. Let's all leave."

"I guess I'm not used to the crowd," he said. "I'll take a walk."

"Why don't we take a couple of beers and sit out on the dock?" said Sam.

Dan looked awkwardly at Dorothy who laughed, showing brilliant white teeth and pink tongue. "I'd join you, but I guess my presence wouldn't be appreciated," she said.

"Please join us," said Sam.

"OK, I'll get something to drink then." Dorothy went off to the other end of the hall and Dan said, "What's up with her?"

"Don't you want her to come?"

"Sure, but she's really uptight."

"She's pregnant. And she's lonely. The guy who got her pregnant worked for the government here. He's in Ottawa now."

"And she's getting married?"

"Well, she's told everyone he's getting a divorce and she's going to be married. She's going to Ottawa for sure."

"I'm sorry for her."

"She likes you. Why don't you take her out there on the dock and cheer her up a bit?"

"Well, you come, Sam. Then I can talk to you," he said suddenly. "I mean there's lots to say."

"There is?" she laughed again. "I suppose there could be."

Dorothy appeared with a bottle in a paper bag, and some plastic cups.

"Let's go. I got something special."

She went towards the screen door. Sam said, "Oh Dan, I'd like you to meet Rod and this is Cunard." She introduced Dan.

Dan shook hands, taking a close look into the pudding face of Rod. He waved at Cunard who was standing behind Rod. They both smelt heavily of drink.

"C'mon," said Dorothy. "Why don't you join us, Rod?"

"Is that booze?" He pointed to the bag in Dorothy's hand.

"The best. Only the very best," said Dorothy. "Cunard, are you coming?"

"No. He's got a job to do," said Rod quickly, "but I'll join you."

Down near the water, on the other end of the dock the air was awash with silvers and golds from the sun. It must have been ten o'clock but it was still as light as midday and the only way you could tell it was night was because there was a dampness in the air. They sat on the end of the great wooden platform and Sam took off her shoes and rolled up her jeans. She put her feet slowly into the water, feeling the cold crispen the flesh on her legs. Dorothy threw the paper bag into the water and poured from the bottle into the paper cups. The liquid was hot and raw in Dan's throat.

"Jesus. What is it?" he managed.

Dorothy said, "Gin and home-hooch."

"Ma used to make it if we ran out. Dad was an alcoholic. It's made from boiled potato peelings. Don't drink it if you don't like it, Dan," she said.

"Well, I like it," said Rod, holding out his cup for a refill.

Dan noticed that Dorothy's hand was shaking as she drank. She was on her third now.

Sam was lying back on the dock. Dan decided that Sam was really prettier than Dorothy. Deep down she had a lot more and her eyes were quite beautiful. Sam was in one of her reveries. Rod began to sing loudly, "Oh my darling, oh my darling, oh my darling Clementine . . ."

While Sam had her eyes shut, Dan looked closely at her face, its red lips and the tight skin, parchment-like over the high cheeks. It seemed he had known her a long time. It wasn't the features, of course, he told himself, it was the strange, intimate contact they had had from almost the first moment.

"It's a mining song," Rod said tipsily as if no one had heard the song before. "All the miners sing it."

Dorothy took Dan's arm and squeezed, looking over her shoulder afterwards to make sure Sam hadn't seen. She poured Dan another drink. He was pleasantly disorientated, wanting to be alone with Sam, yet being very attracted by the overtures that Dorothy was making.

"Rod Ziegel, put that goddam bottle down! You've had enough. Go get some of your dad's booze and bring it here," said Dorothy.

Dorothy ran her hand over Dan's thigh. The name Ziegel sobered Dan like a cold shower. So this was Ziegel's son! Christ! He had better be careful.

Dorothy said, "I'd like to go for a boat ride. If I get you some more booze from good old dad's liquor cabinet, we will take a couple of boats out?"

Sam remained lying on her back, her legs slightly parted and her feet still splashing in the water. Her arms were nesting her hair which she had undone and let fall over the dry, hard pine of the dock. Her eyes were slits as she withdrew into herself.

"Go get the fucking drink, Rod, and then we'll get some boats," she said.

Dorothy lifted her face close to Dan's to allow him to kiss her. His cheek brushed her lips.

Rod rose slowly to his feet and leaned over Sam. It angered Dan as Rod put his lips to Sam's. But the anger changed to a smile as Sam's hand came up and hit Rod across the cheek.

"Keep yourself away from me, you bugger," she said, "I've warned you and Cunard about that."

Sam sat up and shook her hair over her shoulders, lighting a cigarette and drawing her knees up so that she could hug them.

Dorothy said, "This time next week, I'll be in my Ottawa apartment. Vincent says it faces the Rideau canal—that must be near the main drag, I guess."

"You've never been to Ottawa?" said Dan.

"I've never been to Ottawa, Toronto, Montreal or Vancouver. My parents live here. I was born here and I've been as far as Edmonton. But they say Ottawa is very pretty. The apartment has two bedrooms, one for Vincent and me and another for the baby. So if you guys come as guests you'll have to sleep on the sofa."

Dorothy poured the last of the home-made hooch into her cup and said, "Vincent is a very important man in Ottawa. He's a geologist with the government. And we are going to be married in a church that stands behind the parliament buildings. I've seen pictures of it. And by that time . . ." Her voice temporarily trailed away. She was past summoning the energy to finish.

Sam said, "Dorothy, why don't you lie down and have a sleep . . ."

"You just don't want to hear my story," Dorothy said. She put her head on Dan's shoulder and slipped her arm into his shirt, rubbing his chest as if it were a pillow.

"You are just jealous because Dan here likes me and because I'm going to be married," she went on. "And, Sam, when are you going to leave us and go back to the party . . .?"

"Oh, shut up," said Sam dreamily and softly. Dan took Dorothy's hand out of his shirt and replaced it in her lap . . . Dorothy's eyes went towards the water.

"Lovely, lovely water. I'd like to jump in and to swim to my Vincent . . ." She stopped and looked up at Dan with her face like a child's only inches from his lips. Sam was sitting again now.

"Lay off him," she said. "Dorothy, knock it off."

"When you both come to see us in Ottawa, Vincent will show you his children. I haven't seen them yet. Only in pictures. But he's got a divorce now and Sheila and Brenda will visit us on weekends."

"For Christ's sake, Dorothy, shut up." Sam had had enough. She got up and tried to pull Dorothy to her feet.

Rod came back with a bottle of imported gin and another of Scotch.

Dorothy stood up leaning on Sam's arm, but it was too much for her. She sat again heavily and Rod poured out another round of drinks. Dorothy took Dan's hand and kissed it, completely ignoring Sam in her drunkenness.

"Dan, you and me—we'll go out in the boat together?"

Dan looked at her. "I think you should go home."

"And you and her'll go out together, Dannyboy?" pouted Dorothy.

Rod said, "I got a boat. There's no kicker, but I managed to get a couple of paddles. Guess you can handle a paddle?" There was a tone to his voice that Dan didn't like. But he held his tongue.

Dorothy said, "Are you not going to take me in the boat, Dan?" She held out her arm for him to pick her up and then dropped it down his right leg onto his foot. "Please take me."

Rod said, "I'll look after her. Don't worry. You two go out in the boat. It's clear of *mozzies* out there. Should be a nice ride. Here, take this. Compliments of my dad." He handed over the bottle of Scotch.

Rod, Sam and Dan left Dorothy singing quietly to the water and they walked down to the shore, past Fatty's place which was now unbearably noisy. There, Rod left them. "I'd better go and see to her."

"You see she gets home, Fatso, or else . . ." said Sam.

"You bet. Don't worry about her. The boat's over there. Someone's put it in the water for you." He waved. "Dorothy," he shouted, "Dorothy, come on back to Fatty's. I'll get you a drink."

Sam took Dan's hand. "Thank you for coming with me, Dannyboy," she said. "Sorry about that scene with Dorothy, she's in a terrible state."

"Which boat is it?" said Dan, not expecting an answer for they could now see it.

A big man was sitting on the stern, smoking a cigarette. As they drew near, Sam took his hand again and her body came closer and warm at his side.

At the boat's stern Sam said, "Hi, Andy. Is it your boat?"

"Yep. Ain't no kicker, but I got a couple of paddles."

Andy stood up. They climbed in and Dan took a paddle to back-slash the boat away from the shore, but Andy gave it a push which Dan noticed sent it yards out.

Sam said, "It's cooler even this far out and I'm sobering."

"Who's he?" whispered Dan.

"Not a very nice character. He does odd jobs around town. Rod's probably paid him so we can use the boat."

They fell into a silence while Dan steered the canoe out into the lake. He could see the lonely figure of Dorothy on the end of the dock, trying to kick her legs in the water.

The air had sobered them both and Sam now sat back with her head cushioned in her hands and looked at him.

"What are you thinking?" she asked.

"Just thinking about Dorothy," he said.

"There are some stars coming out. Must be near midnight now."

"The lake looks like silver."

"When the moon comes out here it looks like people dancing on the water," she said.

"I've got a nice canoe at Fort Norman. I like to go out at night."

"To fish?"

"Sometimes. Sometimes for other reasons."

"With girls?"

"Yes." He blushed, remembering a couple of times.

"Yes. I'll bet you do."

"You think I'm a regular kid. Wet behind the ears."

"Sure you are."

"Suppose I told you half the time since I've been here I've been thinking of you." He was glad that the sun was so low now so she couldn't see him. It gave him confidence.

She sat forward, her figure relaxed and attractively soft. She opened the Scotch.

"I'll bet you spend your time thinking of all the women."

"No. I've always had an idea of a certain kind of woman and I think a lot about her."

"Like your mom?" She drank and handed him the bottle. "Don't spill it. It's the real thing."

"No, he said, "as a matter of fact like you." He paused. "Really, I'm serious."

There was a pause. Then she said, "Funny. I believe you. How many times have you been with girls?"

"Oh, several," he lied.

"Several?"

"Yes. But it has to be for real. I have to really like a girl." He coughed through his hand. "And you? I expect you've been with many guys?"

"A few. Never had much luck though. I'm like you. For you, how many really?"

He grinned, "Well, none like you. Honest. No one, Sam."

"Did you want to go to bed with Dorothy back there?"

"I couldn't do it when she was like that."

"I'll bet you could. All men can. It's just another body."

"Maybe. But she's sick. D'you think it was all right to leave her?"

"Yes. Rod'll look after her."

"I don't like Rod. I don't trust him."

"Nor do I, but he'll do it. He's too scared I'll tell around town about him. He's a fag."

"He's not!"

"Well, he's certainly a.c.–d.c."

"You mean both?" he said never having heard the term.

"Yes. He and Cunard. I think Rod's scared of women. He's the sort that likes to see someone else doing it."

She leaned forward in the boat and gave him a peck on the cheek. "I'd better not do any more while you are driving."

He was feeling good now, but he still didn't know what to say. He started to laugh.

"Do you really mean none of them was like me?" she asked.

"I'm serious about it."

"That's good."

She was silent again for a few minutes and he had paddled out for over half a mile. The surface was clear and glass-like. Likely there would be a storm later on. He heard her yawn and mumble to herself that she was tired.

"Want to go back?" he said.

"No," she said enigmatically.

"What does happen to you when you go silent like that?"

"I think about things."

"Things? What things?"

"You are a strange one, Daniel Nelson. Hey, that's not a bad name for a guy who paddles a boat . . ."

Dan put the paddle in the boat and with a quick look at the stars, he came forward on his knees and kissed her on the lips. He was not sure that she would yield but she put up no resistance.

And so he kissed her again. This time for real. Then she said, "Dan, we'd better be getting back," and he knew she meant it. He started to paddle to the shore.

The stars looked clear as gold. She said, "I sometimes think on nights like this, it seems as if God has taken a handful of gold pebbles and thrown them into the sky."

He started to answer her, but she was asleep, so he applied himself to the paddles and made for the shore where he could see that Andy was still keeping watch, because he lit a fire which also glistened through the one hour of night which was blue-black at this time of year.

As the boat touched the shore, Dan stood up and a surprisingly lively Sam jumped out and ran up the bank to the dock. As Dan put his foot onto the shoreline he thought that perhaps she was asking him to run after her and to catch her, but his second, more powerful thought was that she was letting off steam because the feelings in her were as pent up as in him. She was expressing uninhibited exuberance.

He bent to tie the boat and something hit him on the neck. It was a rabbit punch which would have flattened, if not killed, him, had he not slipped with the knot on the boat hitch. As it was the blow hit him near the shoulder. The pain was like a red-hot poker in his collar-bone.

Instinct warned him to keep his head low and to use his left to feint for a right. He brought the right up from the tips of his toes, with all the art that old Father Binamet, who had been Belgian amateur heavyweight champion, had taught him, into the man's guts.

In spite of the drink and the late hour, the blow was accurate and it carried a lot of weight with it. He felt it go home into the man's solar plexus. As he pulled back he covered his face with his right elbow and drew back his left arm which was in surprisingly good shape.

The man let out a yell. It was Andy. Dan felt a stinging blow to the left side of his head and then another in his groin as he seemed to be hit with a piece of wood. He started to ward off another right, but his head spun. His legs went weak and blow after blow landed on his chest, knocking the wind out of him and causing him to fall to his knees.

A knee came up under his chin and he was knocked on his back. He hit the rockface with a thud which echoed through his body. He lay there for a fraction of a second hoping to get back his wind, but a knee came onto his chest and a hand went down into his shirt, searching for his secret packet. He was being frisked! He looked up into the man's face and saw the hanging flesh around his mouth, the eyes, slitted through the high cheeks and heavy brows.

Dan summoned all the strength in him. He brought up his foot and jammed it into the man's face. The kick clicked under the jaw and the man gave another yell. Dan bounded to his feet. The man yelled yet again as he kicked him in the groin.

Out of the left corner of his eyes, Dan could see some people come running down the rocky path towards him. In the front was Sam. She was screaming blue murder.

He hit with a left jab and then a right hook. He brought his knee up again. But he knew that his strength was gone. The man's reach was much better than his, and the man had incredible stamina. He felt a left, then a right and another right, come home and he heard the crunch in his jaw as the last right went home. He took a wild wide swipe and then saw the man's knife. It was under his throat.

A hand came over the man's shoulder and someone pulled him away. It was Cunard. Rod stood behind.

A crowd had gathered. Someone was patting his face with a cloth. It was Sam. The cloth was torn from her blouse. She was crying and trying to kiss him at the same time as she wiped the blood from his face.

Three guys from Fatty's led Andy away, and Dan saw him

shake them off with a sweep of his huge arms and run for it through the trees.

"Why did he? Why?" Dan managed. He was still trying to even up his breathing.

Rod said, "He's a bastard. Must have taken a dislike to you, eh, Cunard? My guess is that you should get out of town pronto, man. Like early tomorrow. He's a killer."

Cunard said, "That man Andy is crazy like a bear, Dan. But I tell you he's not goin' ter get you. Me and Rod'll look after you. We'll see to that. Crazy bastard."

Sam said, "Come home. Yes home, Dan. Here, take my arm. All the rest of you, fuck off."

Dan felt her arm go under his and then he blacked out.

Cunard and Rod helped Sam back to the cabin with Dan. Rod then took Cunard outside giving him more instructions. Then Rod went home to bed. They were asleep when a small party of early morning revellers left Fatty's and walked the lakeshore to see a lump of crumpled clothing floating in the lake. They pulled it out and there was a body underneath. Dorothy had either fallen or jumped into the water. She was alive and asked for a drink.

SEVEN

It was like the noise of an animal, soft and padding. It came from the veranda outside the café. Dan woke sweating with Sam's head on his chest. He tried to twist his neck so that he could see out of the window at the end of the bedroom, where the padding seemed to have become loudest. He thought he could hear grunting too, like someone lifting something. Then Dan realised that there might be several sources of the noise. One out front, perhaps another coming towards the window and yet others, scraping and clawing at some wood.

It could not be racoons or skunks. Might be bears. Yet he didn't smell animals. He smelt humans. He lifted Sam's head off his chest and placed it on the pillow.

Someone had taken off all his clothes and covered him with a sort of towel. The clock beside Sam's bed said ten to two. He hadn't been asleep long. He tried to move off the bed and to make his way to the window. Except for his neck, it seemed he wasn't in too bad shape. But he knew that he hadn't yet had time to stiffen up. Give his muscles another couple of hours and they'd become aching sheets of iron, especially in his chest which right now seemed wet. Half-way off the bed, he froze. There it was again. The noise. Just under the window. Like huge rats. It brought up the hackles on his neck.

He turned to place the towelling on the bed. Sam was stretched out in her jeans, just as she came in. Her thumb was up on the pillow beside her head, as if she had been sucking her fist. She looked a child now. He wondered how she'd had the strength to undress him. He leaned over and took off her shoes, dainty white, heel-less pieces of skimpy leather. How did they support her? Spiders' webs with leather fingers for soles.

There was the noise again. He stood up quickly. Too quickly. His head spun and his back jerked him forward in a hoop. He reached out and with his fingertips caught the door handle. It twisted under his touch and the door swung open revealing the blue pre-dawn light. A shadow flicked through it. Dan wasn't sure, it seemed human but on all fours.

Now that he was moving, the pains lessened and he was able to walk upright. But he knew that in time this too would be agony to even try.

Under the counter, near the chopping board, he'd seen Sam put a bread knife. It was a razor-like instrument, honed thin in the middle and with a deer-horn handle. He reached in for it and finally his hand hit it.

Then the noise outside came again. It was more hurried now. The several noises seemed to have congregated in one place.

Dan's sleepy brain suddenly came to life. The gold! Someone was after the gold. Perhaps many people were after it. He let the towel drop and undid the bolt on the café door. The landscape around him was still in night. Someone was digging where he'd put the stuff. The weird panting was regular now. There must be at least two people it seemed. He cursed himself for staying and he cursed again for getting into that fight.

A town is a living entity in itself and the big news now was his find, so that many would be after him, like rats in a meat locker. He could have sworn that no one saw him bury that gold. But someone must have seen him. That someone collected together others and they too collected others—it was a frightening feeling.

Dan edged his way silently along the veranda, the knife poised. His bare feet rested only on the balls under the toes and his knees were bent—a hunter.

There was no moon and the stars had clouded over, so that no streak of light penetrated the blackness of the shadowed side of the café. His eye caught movement though. Someone was scratching under the bush. It was impossible to make it in one bound. He came forward two steps. He held the knife beside his ear so that his forearm was parallel to the ground. In the darkness he heard someone give a tug at the ground, as if heaving up a heavy object.

Dan pounced, his knife arm still poised ready to strike. A great ball of fur slid from under him and a yelp of pain stopped him bringing down the knife. Kayuk!

"Kayuk, you bloody stupid bastard!"

The animal looked at him and he saw in its mouth was part of the bush which had been torn away to get at the buried treasure. The gold and the letters had been scratched out by the huge paws and now lay in soft earth under the dog's feet. Dan reached down to pick up the three samples and the documents from Ziegel.

"Goddam fool dog. Idiot hound!" he whispered. He would gladly have given the animal a kick in the backside but he didn't want to risk more strain on his muscles. The dog was looking at him trying to tell him something. And in his heart Dan knew that Kayuk had been trying to help. Perhaps! Anyway, he gave the animal the benefit of the doubt.

Dan went round the front of the café and told Kayuk to sit outside the door which he now rebolted inside, placing the gold and letters on one of the café tables.

He made it back to bed just as the sun was hitting the end of the cabin with its new light. Sam was still asleep. It seemed she had not moved. He lay down beside her and pulled the towelling over him again. How many men? How many animals? His imagination had played a dirty trick!

He started to laugh. It was a long time since he had laughed so much. After that, he fell asleep and he never felt his muscles begin to really harden.

EIGHT

Dan smelt bacon and eggs. Now, hours later, almost every part of him ached, but he was also very hungry. Sam's face poked around the door from the café. Her hair was wound in a soft coil at the back and she had tied a bright yellow bandanna over it.

"You look great this morning," he said.

"Keeps my hair out of the cooking. You look awful. Two eggs and brown toast?"

"I feel awful, maybe I should take a walk."

"It's absolutely forbidden," she said. "And besides I want to eat."

"Sure. I'm ready."

She came forward and kissed him lightly on the forehead, with a cup of tea in her hand.

"Drink this and you'll feel better."

"Thanks a lot for last night."

"The eggs are ready," she went on, "and it's a lovely day."

Dan pulled himself onto the side of the bed and swung his

legs painfully over the side.

"What did you put on my chest?" he asked.

"Cold cream. You got skinned. Rod just came round to ask how you were," she shouted from the café, "drove his red car up to the door."

"Bottle of Scotch, red cars, expensive tastes he has."

"There's nothing wrong with expensive tastes," she said.

"Does he come often?"

"Nearly every day. Just for a chat."

"Just a chat?"

"Oh, nothing else. Not Rod. Although he used to be quite good-looking. But he's got fat and watery. Why do you ask?"

Dan levered himself to his feet and stood now with the towelling bathrobe around him at the door. He put his tea to his lips. The heat stung the cuts inside his mouth.

"No reason really. It *is* a nice day. Ouch!" Dan lowered himself into a chair and ran his fingers over the three gold samples.

"There's a rich man in Rod Ziegel," he added.

"Money's not everything."

"Sure counts for a lot with girls."

"Not enough to make me want to strike out with someone like Rod," she said, placing a plate in front of him. "What are those rocks?"

"Gold samples," he said. And he told her the story.

"You should have told me. I've got a safe in here."

"Didn't think of it."

She could tell from his voice that he had not trusted her. She was hurt, but she understood. "Does that mean you'll be rich too?"

"You bet your life," he said with some bravado.

"Why would anyone want to steal rocks with gold in them? What could they do with them?"

"Lots. Every vein of gold is like a person—different."

She was looking at him over the top of her cup, her eyes mirroring the sky. It was going to be hard leaving her this morning but he knew he must. There was no place in his plans for a girl, even a girl like Sam. He was thinking that one day he might regret this, but right now he couldn't let it get in the way of his plans.

"If they took the gold to a government assay officer he'd tell them what area it came from. Each vein has its own characteristics, like a painting or carving."

"They they could try to beat you to stake the claim?"

"Yes. It's been done many times before."

It was still very early and they sat for nearly twenty minutes alone enjoying being together. Then she said, "You don't have to go today, do you?"

"Yes. I do."

"You've been pretty badly beaten up . . ."

"All the more reason to go. Someone's already after me. Maybe more than one person. That Andy is a killer."

"So they say."

She was smoking now and the cigarette smoke curled up through her fingers and into her hair, giving her a soft misty look. They sat again for a while and he took her cup and refilled it. She saw his swollen right knuckles and clasped his hand in between her hands. "Please don't go today. Rest. Come for a walk."

"I'd like to. You know that. But I can't. This is very important to me," he said pointing at the gold.

"Is it really?" she said. "Then tell me about it, Dan."

He started to tell. "Not far from me, across the Mackenzie, in the mountain foothills, there's an old trail. Jonas Barnes from Fort Norman used to take me there as a kid of 12. Hunting and trapping. The trail cuts through the mountains about a hundred and fifty miles north-west of us, only you can't see it because it curves behind the foothills and seems to end in a small lake. But it's not a lake, it's a plateau, about ninety-five miles wide, and flat as a plate. It's worse than the Barrens in winter."

Dan hesitated and sipped his tea. She was looking at him

oddly and he smiled.

"I'll bet you're thinking what a fool I am."

"No. I'm listening," she said eagerly.

"Two winters ago I got stuck on the far side of the plateau. My dogs packed it in. And I had no food left . . ."

"What did you do?"

"I shot a dog and ate it . . ."

"You cooked a dog?"

"I ate it raw," he said. "It saved my life." He paused again and noticed she had taken his hand in hers once more.

"I eventually found this cave about three miles into the mountains. Bears had been in it and it was shitty. I was there a week waiting for the storm to pass over . . . And I saw the back of the cave sloped up. I stood on the surface and climbed up. But my feet slipped under me. There was wet moss under the ice. I turned on my flashlight. Honestly, Sam. I was standing on a solid slab of gold. Big as this goddam café. So I took out my hammer and knife and chipped away the samples." He touched them on the table for a second.

"Then what happened? How'd you make it back?"

"The weather eased up and I found my way, but I lived off that dog and the frozen moss for ten days."

"How did you know the gold was so good?"

"You can tell. I took a piece to Father Binamet at Fort Norman and he said I needed grub-staking." He paused bouncing the gold rock up and down in his palm, like a baseball. She had lit another cigarette. The sun was well up now and heating his back. It felt good.

"Father Binamet told you to come to Ziegel?"

"Hell no! He was against it. But he said it was my decision, not his. Ziegel's got the money to develop it for me—and besides—I went back and found another. I've never told anyone about that. Certainly not Ziegel. I'll stake it for myself. No one except me can find that. With a bit of luck, I'll end up rich as Rockefeller or whoever . . ."

They both laughed shyly and intimately.

"Truly, I've never told anyone—but you, Sam."

"I believe you. I'm glad you did. But be careful."

"I can look after myself."

"Men and gold are bad mixtures. They say they breed disease."

"I'm all right, honest."

"I'm scared for you, Dan. Don't get the fever."

"Not me. I'll stay off both claims for as many days as I have to to shake off anyone who comes after me. I'll stake it alone. I've got that much determination. I get it from my grandmother."

"Well, I suppose you know." She put out her hand. "I'll wish you all the best then!"

They sat again in silence, this time occasionally glancing at each other and then glancing away, like children discovering each other's faces. Then Dan took his torn clothes from the stove where Sam had put them to dry and pulled them on over his wounds.

"Sure you won't stay?" she repeated.

"Why?" he asked with a directness that unnerved her.

"God knows why. I just feel it."

"It's a long way down to my home," he said.

"You coming back?"

"I told you right here last night. Yes, I'm coming back."

"I'd like to see you again," she managed, holding back her emotions.

He was pleased she had said it. "I'll be back sooner than you think," he said. "Give me another mug of tea, then I'll be out of your way! It's a great day for a journey."

NINE

Rod Ziegel still lived with his father, and the two were having breakfast at the Mermaid Café on the corner of 4th and Main Streets. It was an unlikely place for Ted Ziegel to be, but well chosen because of that.

After he had told the story of the previous night, Rod looked at his father. "You want me to take Cunard with me?"

"Only a goddam Indian is any use in the bush, son. For Christ's sake, don't take Andy. Don't even let him know. He's too dangerous."

"Then how do we cut Cunard in?"

"That's up to you. He's your protection. Things aren't what they used to be with Indians. Some of 'em have got pretty smart lawyers now. And Ottawa's always been partial to a bit of Indian-loving."

"I like the guy, Dad," said Rod, "he's keeping watch on the café for us now."

"So be fair."

Rod's eyes were still heavy from lack of sleep and the beef

red of his face had streaked into the pupils. His father continued, "This is a business deal. I'll be in at the start and I'll come back at the finish. But in between I can't risk being seen to be in it. It's all up to you, Rod."

In another part of town, not far from Sam's café, Andy was loading a rifle, readying his supplies for a hunt. In the lobby of the Eskimo Inn, men in business suits were waiting for phone calls from Toronto where the business day was well started. In the local brokerage of Doherty and Brown there were whispers. At the *Yellowknife News*, Karl Hinston was doing a story. His speciality was gossip. And out of the back alleys and dirt-lined, treeless bush came the dregs of the world, those who live in the North like rats and unseen animals of the night, until they hear magic words which drag them out. The word above all other being mentioned that morning was gold.

And in Sam's café, through the shyness, a great friendship was growing, unsoiled and unimpeded by too many words. Then there was a scratch at the screen door. Sam rose and opened it to let in the dog. She bent over him. "He's like a huge tree-trunk that someone's covered in a bear's skin," she said.

"What are you going to do with him?" she said.

"Me? He's your dog."

"Maybe he'll stay around." She paused and stood up, throwing the scrapings from the plate onto the veranda for him. "You are right, it is a lovely day to start a journey, or something," she said.

"I'll be back before freeze-up," he reassured her.

"Guess so."

"What's that on the veranda?" he asked.

"Some bacon I threw out for Kayuk."

"No." Dan rose quickly and then she heard him laughing outside the door. "Come and take a look."

When she went out he was pointing to a small fist-sized bundle of old shirt still wet from Kayuk's mouth. "The bugger must have dug it up while we were asleep. Dan wrapped the gold and documents in the old shirt again. It seemed it was a token, a symbol.

"I'll get some more tea," Sam said, and went inside. She strove to think of a way to make him stay longer, just one more day.

When he eventually came in for the tea, she was no further ahead with the thought. She had lost that battle.

She packed him some food, staples like flour for bannock, beans and eggs. Some tea-bags and sugar. Meanwhile, he bent over the table in her small room, fondling the rocks. They were even more precious now. Yet he had already developed a hate for them, because they were precious and therefore dangerous. There is in every man the wishful seed that his gold would turn out to be gold of luck, warmth and happiness. Dan could not get that thought from his mind. It stuck. It overrode the temptation to throw the samples down the hill and watch them fall into small pieces.

Sam knew what he was thinking as he sat there. She put her arm round his shoulder and acted out the only part she could play right now, that of a fond sister.

Nature sends such luck as Dan apparently had come upon, only once in a lifetime. Fate itself offers it to us and Fate itself will make it what it wills. Man can only follow his instinct and hope that Fate will be kind to him. That is why it is often better to be poor and free than to become rich and a slave to yourself, thought Dan.

When the moment finally came for them to part, Dan vowed he would walk out as he came in, unattached. He liked Sam too much, and he knew he could hardly bear that searching in her eyes.

He hitched the pack with the groceries in it onto his back. She came arms nervously akimbo, to the edge of the small veranda, saying nothing as she often did.

"Don't worry about me. I'll be back," he repeated.

"Yes. Well, come soon. Write or phone or something."

"Sure. The phones are in at home now. We've five in town," he laughed.

Dan could see the dog, crouching doggo on the rock over the end of the veranda.

"Why don't you take him with you?"

"They'd shoot him at Fort Norman. There's too much wolf in him."

The last thing he wanted to do was saddle himself with another possession. The next few months, he was going to have to work by himself, unencumbered. The dog was not taking its eye off him though, a smouldering piece of charcoal, red around the edge and hot on Dan.

Sam put her arms around Dan and he found himself asking why didn't he just take the girl to bed? She was kissing him and one small tug towards the door and he would have weakened. But that never came.

And when Dan finally waved good-bye at the brow of the hill, she was still standing there. He paused to watch her wave back. Then she picked up a broom and started with long strong strokes to sweep the dust off the veranda.

At the foot of the rocks, he turned again. He could just see the chimney of the café. A thin black thread of smoke circled into the crystal air.

As his eyes came down again to his own level, he caught sight of the dog. He was standing so still that he was hard to see among the rust colour of the rocks.

"Go back." He picked up a rock and hurled it, not caring if he hurt the animal or not. The rock bounced aimlessly by the creature and he came two steps nearer and again stood like a statue.

"Goddam you. You idiot. Go back to Sam," Dan shouted.

The dog slowly cocked its head on one side and licked its lips.

Dan turned and began to walk quickly. By the time he reached the pines at the edge of the stream, he found the dog only paces behind. "Go home," he shouted. "Go home, you fucking sonofabitch."

Why did the dog make him feel so angry? He picked up a

rock and pretended to throw it. The dog's eyes flicked only. He threw the rock. This time he was sure he would hit it. It was travelling fast. The dog was twenty feet away. But the dog was faster. He merely shifted his weight onto his right paw and let the rock pass. Then, still with his ears at the alert and his tongue tucked tightly inside his jaw, the dog lowered himself to his lying position, all without taking his eyes off Dan.

Dan turned angrily on his heel and began to run. He reached the small river and jumped the pools in which fresh lake herring swam and bounded into the bush on the other side. Confident that the dog would not now follow he ran up the hill and looked back at the town. You could see all the old town from this spot. He wondered if Sam had finished sweeping the veranda.

It was a fine day in the bush. It was perfect. The sky was a velvet rug, just a few shades lighter than Sam's eyes. The rocks met it in the foreground like crystals of sheer copper, and the bush around smelt of honey, the night dew and the fresh droppings of animals. This was home to Dan. It spoke to him, telling him things, straight, simple things. Beautiful or ugly, bare or rich in clothing, soothing or aggressive. The mosquitoes and blackflies were not yet out, from the creepers under which they took refuge at night.

Below to his left lay the huge river. Men had told him that next to the Amazon, there wasn't one much bigger. Behind the Mackenzie were the foothills of the mountains that bore the same name. On the other side, to his back, lay the Barrens, lands which stretched much further than the eye could see, as flat as a table and it was here that men died. But they also died in the mountains.

Dan looked down. The dog had crossed the creek. He was sitting twenty feet away, still watching him. The sight made him furious. He turned and walked another two feet. He stopped and turned. The dog too was still, his head more relaxed as if he were about to enjoy a game and his tongue, black as the ace of spades, lolling from the side of his mouth.

Dan walked again, this time nonchalantly, and seemingly without purpose, but suddenly swivelling on his right foot and staring at the dog who had come close enough now to seem to be grinning at him. Dan couldn't help laughing. The dog gave a sharp, begging bark. Then he bounded forward.

"Get back, you bloody animal, you stupid goddam wolf," Dan screamed, the anger suddenly surprising him in his throat. But the animal playfully bounded nearer.

They were now about a mile from the mainstream of the big river and standing on a sort of plateau, swampy and filled with rattlers in summer, wolves in winter. You could tell they were wolves because of the heaps of bones, the results of their feasting, drying white in the sun.

Dan stopped slowly and picked up a handful of rocks. He supposed now that his anger had something to do with Sam, and the way they had parted. He had wanted to give himself time to forget the girl and the dog was a reminder.

He hurled the first stone and it bit into the rock not a foot in front of the dog. The dog saw the other stones and even as the second came, he jumped in the air and in one bound was in among the trees, standing so still, not even Dan could see him. Guessing where he was Dan threw the rest of the stones and with each shot he sent a curse. Then with the last one gone, he stood waiting. Within seconds the nose of the dog appeared round a rock in the bush, then one paw and finally the whole big animal, like the part wolf that he was, noble and unbeatable. Dan picked up rocks and hurled them wildly, never hitting the dog.

For the next few minutes it was as if he had gone into some sort of fit. There was a strong evil in him, an urge to kill. And the dog was on the other end of the vibrations.

In panic, Dan began to run towards the river, without stopping and yelling his head off in wild, unidentifiable screams. He knew the dog was following, like the spirit of his ancestors, like a demon of the river.

The panic only subsided when he reached the bank of the

river and threw his head into the water, shaking it like some crazy animal until the fever left him. He must have lain there, breathing only by turning his head and then plunging into the cold water again, for at least ten minutes. When he looked up the dog was beside him, drinking, his ears back and his tail, wolf-like, lying along the ground. Dan put up his arm and hugged the dog across the shoulders. He felt the huge tail start to wag. There was nothing to be said. The dog had won. *Kayuk.* Big brown dog.

Dan lay on the bank and fell asleep, deeply and exhausted. He was completely unaware of what had made him panic into madness, just as he was totally unaware of what had happened to Sam since he left.

TEN

Cunard was now very drunk, but he was lucid. He had been told by Rod to keep watch on Sam's cabin since they had both watched Sam help the beaten, bleeding Cree into it and close the door.

At that time Rod had disappeared to bed in the new town, leaving a two-four-pack of Labatt's 50 Ale in Cunard's safe keeping.

When Sam locked the cabin door, the sound made Cunard angry. He would long also have disappeared into the night but Rod was his white buddy and he paid off.

All night long, Cunard let the anger simmer as he drank the beer. He hoped that one day Sam would become his girl and he would come to live in the café, enjoying her and the food, a benevolent middle-class landlord in his fantasy. He had watched Sam ever since she had arrived back in town. Whenever she was around, his eyes were rarely off her. They knew every part of her body, yet they had not yet seen any of it. And for this very reason the ache to see it became an angry hunger.

At times the mere sight of Sam made all other thoughts pass away and one glance from her eyes was enough to arouse him to an almost uncontrollable pitch. There were plenty of other girls around, many of whom slept with him regularly, flirted with him and wanted him enough to become his woman. Why Sam? It was a question he could not answer.

He rattled the case of now empty beer bottles. He picked up a bottle in his left hand and flung it down the rocks. It gave him little satisfaction. His imagination became even more vivid with the mixture of heavy rising hatred and the legacy of the beer. He saw the Cree Indian, Dan, in bed with Sam, and then again he saw Sam kissing the Cree the way he often imagined she would stroke him. He saw them in each other's arms and he also saw the sympathy Sam would be lavishing on the man. In a terrifying mixture of emotions he couldn't even begin to understand or to clarify, Cunard was urging himself to go down from his hiding-place to the cabin and to look through the back window, to listen at the lock to enjoy the very sights which were exciting him to hatred. The urging came a hundred times during the long night, and it grew harder and harder in him.

In between these bursts of unconquerable need he turned his anger and hate on the other things in his life he had come to loathe. The fear of the Cree, inbred in Slavey people, was one of them. Another was Yellowknife itself but most important was the fact that he had been born an Indian. No one could ever take that away. He had heard that even in New York and Toronto, the white man would spot you and point you out. Strangely, Cunard didn't hate the white man for this. He hated himself. It was as strong as his feelings about the Cree, whose throat he was tempted to cut as soon as he came out of the cabin.

But Cunard, like most of his race, was a fatalist and in spite of such fancies, he did not unsheathe his knife when Dan came out this morning, kissing Sam good-bye and wandering down the rocks with the dog on his heels. His fatalism led him to wait;

to withhold the action. The time was not ready.

He let his eyes walk across the figure of Sam, stroking her back and thighs as she bent to brush the porch. And watching her fingers playing on the handle of the broom as she moodily replaced it. Cunard took out his knife, fingered it and replaced it too. Then he stood up.

Sam looked up casually from behind the counter as he came in. She smiled and he could see the sadness in her eyes. She looked down again quickly.

"You got a little time now, Sam?" Cunard said. His tone should have warned her, but it didn't. She had been alone with Cunard many times. He frightened her with his strange, hard looks, but she could deal with him.

"Coffee with double cream, Cunard?" she said without even looking up.

"Wrong. Dead wrong," he said.

This time she was startled at his voice. She looked up slowly. "No coffee," he repeated, grinning at her. Now she was frightened. Her hand went down the counter for the bread knife. She fumbled to the left and missed it. Dan had put it back in a different place.

Cunard grabbed her wrist and pulled it onto the counter. Her shoulder came forward against his chest and she felt him push hard against her as she fell back against the shelves.

"Now take it easy. If you make a sound, I'll really hurt you. Be a good girl and you won't get hurt."

Sam saw the tightness of the skin of his cheeks and the hard set of his jaw. She felt again the weight of his body. Then she must have fainted.

The men from the mine found her half an hour later. She was still lying behind the counter. She was in shock and crying constantly. They took her off in the foreman's car to the hospital where the doctors confirmed what had happened. It was one of a dozen or so cases they saw every week. This was a frontier town, on one of the world's last frontiers.

But by the time she had been allowed to go home at her own

insistence, Cunard was on his way north to Fort Norman with Rod to await the arrival of Dan. And she never told them who it was who had raped her. It was wiser not to tell, she figured. She was to prove herself right.

ELEVEN

The great river was almost a mile wide at this point, but a few hundred yards ahead it snaked suddenly west, so that the shore-line was in the dark blue shadow of the mountains and even the outlines of the poplars and bush trees which grew matted along the river banks were coal-coloured.

The prow of the canoe slipped into sight as Dan was about to put a match to a pile of twigs. The thick, steel-edged outline of Andy, hunched forward like a long hatchet, his hands almost reaching the water with each stroke, dipping deep and pulling in long silent rhythms, startled Dan. His own heart was all he could hear.

He put his hand over the dog's mouth. But the animal never flinched. Its eyes were on the canoe, which was again moving towards the black silence of the trees, its silhouette catching, for a second, the silver of the moonlit water, highlighting Andy's rifle resting on the prow. The canoe disappeared as silently as it came, and Dan breathed freely, rubbing his hand under the dog's chin. The animal cocked its head towards

Dan's and Dan was glad of the warmth of the body pulled to his side. The dog gave him a feeling of home and security, but it was not strong enough to take away the fear which had come in a dry coating in his mouth at the sight of Andy so close behind.

He told himself that he had always expected this. A thousand times he had gone over it in his mind even before making the trip to Yellowknife. There was going to be trouble. This was as sure as the breath he drew. People were desperate, not from poverty, although there was enough of that around, but from sheer greed. It ran like a poison through his people, a poison introduced originally by the white man. Everything had its price. Every man could be bought. But these facts only made Dan more determined.

This was his land, belonging through ages to his people. It had been raped and pillaged, its plunder filling the coffers of the great banks in Toronto and New York, but what Dan had found, he had a right to. It was what the land gave up to him. A sort of reward, like a good harvest or a plentiful trapline. And this gave him a strength he never knew he had. It was what had pushed him on into Ziegel's office. He was sure. And proud that he was right. It made him know that, in spite of the inevitable trouble, he would stake his claims.

Dan hadn't thought much about killing up to that point. Just that killing was wrong. Maybe even stupid. Plenty of killings took place in every settlement in the North. Life was raw and people lived much by old laws, old truths. Death was cheap and life very dear, especially your life.

But, Dan told himself, people had never seen the whole of him. The talk from his elder brother, from his mother, was that he was the sort of man made to be a priest or a teacher. A man of peace, whose stalk waved gently, not standing stiff against the wind. Perhaps only Father Binamet knew for sure. Ever since he could remember the old priest had been his confessor.

None the less, Dan kept much of himself to himself. The priest said, "Justice is not to be found much in this world.

Don't let your mind hanker after it. It can become a career."

Dan understood what he meant. Deep down, under the skin of his thoughts he knew that he would do a lot for revenge. Revenge was capable of overwhelming him. From the day when as a boy, barely 9, he had come home and, while his mother pinioned his arms, he had tried to fight off two white men who had beaten his father almost to the point of death in a drunken brawl. Revenge was sweet food, which gave him an almost insatiable appetite, an appetite only dampened by the music of the bush he loved to spend his days in.

The dog's nose, pushing wet under his hand, took him from his thoughts. He discovered that in his reverie he had crushed the poor, small pile of twigs to heat his supper into sticks no bigger than matches. His left hand, darkly veined and muscular, now held the small pack of food which Sam had packed.

He opened some beans and poured half out for the dog which ate them voraciously. He ate quickly himself, not wanting to risk a fire. He mopped the plate clean with a piece of Sam's heavy, home-made bread and then sat on his haunches, his arms swinging lightly over his knees, as he munched some cheese and let his thoughts start to wash over him again.

The dog licked its paws, lying grey against the soil, almost a log, and then retreated to the bush. For a time, Dan watched its eyes, the only visible part as they seemingly searched his. He threw a piece of cheese, and heard a jaw snap over it.

To reach Fort Norman it would take him at least another four days' walking. He clutched the small rocky package closer to his chest. Normally it would have been better to travel at night, and he was geared up enough to move, but he was not sure of this stretch of river and he thought, because of Andy, he would go even deeper into the bush to the east to skirt the river bend. Andy was hardly likely to take the canoe through the bush.

The night was now all around him like a blanket, yet it seemed it was not like night. The night seemed to be staying awake, like day, despite the heaviness in his eyes and the aches in his limbs, and he too was able to forget these pains in his determination.

Once he got to Fort Norman it did not mean that his troubles would be over. On the contrary, he was expecting the news to have arrived ahead of him and the settlement to have divided itself into little groups, some of them planning against him. For this reason he was also determined not to start laying claims to the discoveries until he was ready. He might not even leave until after Christmas. He certainly wouldn't set out right now. It was tempting fate to do so. In any case it would be best to wait for the first snow and he'd surely go alone. To hit the trail in summer meant travelling round lakes and trying to navigate muskeg. Freeze-up came in mid-September. That was six weeks away. Winter was travel time in the Arctic. Few men risked it in summer, especially if they wanted to cover up their trails. On the great river, for instance, you could take a snowmobile nearly two thousand miles up it in winter if you skirted the rapids.

There were no paths, no roads, few marks of men in the lush tangle of twisted trees and shrubs. White men and strangers to the river got lost here, one tree leading to another until people dropped from exhaustion.

Tomorrow, with the sun behind him, when Dan cut into the back of the bush and worked his way around Andy, it would be hard going, but the distance he would travel would be shorter, for the river zigzagged its way north.

The dawn came finally in a great wash of low-level light, and Dan, who had already eaten, started immediately, the dog trotting at his heels.

He whistled to himself, thinking about Sam, repeating her name in full and in short form. When it was all over and he had money, he would buy her something. It would have to be something she had always wanted and could never afford. He couldn't forget her eyes. He wished he had stayed longer with her and vowed that if he met her again, he would.

The going was slow. Heavy wet moss, long dangerous patches of permafrost, a muddy deep layer of swampy material, peculiar to the Arctic, which froze in hillocks in winter, raising the corners of buildings as high as three feet in the air, and in summer sank into a seemingly bottomless quagmire.

The air was infested with mosquitoes. Every leaf seemed alive. Even the dog was being bitten, stopping every few yards to turn and bite his own rear-end to ease the itching. Soon Dan spotted a rise ahead, topped with barren rock and grossly stunted pine. He must be getting near the tree line.

He knew he was not home. But at least at the top of the rise, he would get a slight breeze which would blow the mosquitoes away, and he would see the river again.

The rise was a bed of rock, not unlike a table. The trees that grew on it were in small hollows where water had once collected and where the winds had blown in dust. Dan walked to the edge, easing the pack off his shoulder and trying vainly not to scratch his mosquito bites. Below in a leisurely sweep north was the Mackenzie.

He had been walking for three hours. He was thirsty and hungry. For a few seconds he surveyed the scene for signs of movement or fire. It seemed there wasn't a man in a thousand miles. He picked up the pack and started down the steep, stony slope to the small plateau, studded with poplars, wild trilliums and lily of the valley, which went to the water's edge. The dog followed, sliding and grumbling in sharp barks. Arctic foxes made their homes in the side of the slope. Their droppings were exciting the dog.

At the bottom, Dan ran to the water and drank. It was good, clear, and it increased his hunger. He undid the pack and from the side pocket took out a line. He baited it with the piece of fat ham left over from the beans. When he was sure that the line was draped to catch the current along the slow-moving waters near the bank where the bass would lie, he tied the end to a branch and gathered a few sticks for a fire.

Twenty minutes later he was eating, the dog lying back from

him about fifty feet away in the shade, waiting for the remains.

The animal was patient and intelligent. Dan had grown used to having him. He tried to push from his mind the thought that he would probably have to shoot him when he got to Fort Norman. The tribal council had passed a by-law. When the snowmobile had taken the dog's place as a worker, the dogs in town had lain around and bred. Many had become dangerous and Chief Chuck Andrews had ordered all strays to be shot. Dan knew now that he wouldn't have the heart to kill the dog.

Dan had finished eating now, the gold samples lying beside him and his mind back on his surroundings. He looked up.

Andy was standing ten feet away. The tip of his rifle was pointed at Dan's head. Andy's eyes were on the rocks. Andy told him to stand up.

TWELVE

It was not the first time that Dan had found himself looking down the barrel of a shotgun, and he was not much afraid, but he was frustrated at his own foolishness.

"Scared the shit out of you," said Andy.

Dan nodded. He was wishing the gold samples were back inside his shirt, instead of lying bare to the sun and to Andy's gaze.

"Just keep standing, lad." Andy sat on his haunches and stood the gun between his legs, using the barrel to steady himself. "Yes. Keep standing that way, until I get through. Don't want any misunderstandings."

"Been watching you. Didn't think I'd seen you, did you?" Andy laughed. "Saw you catch the fish and give some to that dog. Saw you take out the gold and look at it. Saw you go and take a pee and then watched you washing the gold in the river. I been watching you, Dan." He paused and spat out something he had prised loose from his tooth. "And I ain't the only one watching you, Dan. Least I don't think so." He laughed again, the grin wrinkling the pockmarks on his cheeks. Then he said slowly, "Now that's not news to you, is it?"

Out of the corner of his eye, Dan saw the dog, crouching in the bush.

Dan said, "By now I guess half the river knows."

"Ziegler sent out Rod and Cunard to watch you. They're on their way. I heard about it up river, there."

"How about you?"

"I came like a good guy, good friend. You need a friend." Andy's eyes ran over the gold samples. "Looks like you found yourself a mine. Goin' to prove I'm your friend." He threw the rifle on the grass between them. "That prove it?"

Dan never moved. His eyes were bearing into the Pole's face.

"I'm here to protect you from getting killed by some smart guy. You ever heard about Forest Jay?"

"At Simpson?"

"I killed him with this very rifle here. Just as he was getting out of his canoe. Want to know why?"

Dan kept his eyes fixed on the old Pole.

"That was a set-up, too. Like with you the other night. Ziegel done it, too. That man is mean. But, Forest, he toppled out of that canoe and into the river. Never came to the surface again. Had lead in his pockets. Found him hundred miles downstream near where the Laird comes in, they said."

Dan knew if he waited long enough, Andy would relax his vigil. All it needed was to see a flick of his eyes, a muscle moving in his arm or neck. Dan could then act.

"You are not a killer. I am," Andy said. "I'm sticking with you. I'm friend. You won't get rid of me. You register the claim. Then I'll take my cut. It is simple, no?"

His eyes still on Dan, Andy leaned forward onto his knees and made a sudden grab at the rifle. Even before his hand hit the barrel, Dan saw the dog jump. The animal had been crouching, creeping near enough to make it in one bound. The leap was noiseless.

The dog landed on Andy's back and sent him sprawling on his face, his arms spread-eagled. He immediately twisted onto his back. The dog was already on his chest.

"Get him off," he yelled. "Jesu-Maria! Get him off."

Dan rose to his feet and picked up the rifle.

In a panic, Andy tried to hold the dog by the neck tightening his great hands in a stranglehold.

Dan jumped for the animal's neck fur. He yanked the animal back. Andy's right hand thumped into the dog's ribs as it snatched free. With a yelp of pain, it came snarling back at Andy's throat.

Andy cried out and the cry turned to terror as the dog sank its teeth into the flesh. Dan hurled himself on it again, and he managed to tear open the jaws. But the dog broke loose again, and Andy put up his arm only to find the dog's teeth in his elbow. He brought his right arm up and round in a semi-circle into the dog's ribs again. This time the animal never flinched at the pain. The blow knocked Dan back on his side and Andy managed to get to his feet. He swung low with his left arm and caught up the rifle which lay four feet away.

Once again he turned it on Dan. Blood was running down his neck and his arms. There was a razor slash cut in his forehead and a tear in the skin under his left eye.

Andy swung again at the dog, this time with the rifle. He fired. The dog jumped into the air and fell. Dan sprang. But he was too late. The butt of the rifle hit him on the jaw and he felt a hot poker searing into his shoulder. His head hit the earth.

He heard Andy. "I'll watch you, Indian man! You see. I've got you covered from now on."

Out of the corner of his eye Dan saw the dog leap up on one back leg and throw Andy forward onto his chest. As the dog landed the rifle went off again, and something hit him. It was like a car running into his shoulder.

When Dan woke his eyes focused on the moon. He turned his left shoulder wet with blood. The bullet had ripped at the flesh in his arm, by his right shoulder. He dragged himself up.

He looked himself over. Apart from the shoulder he seemed in one piece.

The dog lay in a crumpled heap. He crawled over and touched it gently. It was like something he had caught in a trap. He tilted the head towards him. The eyes were open but lifeless. The nose was cold, yet there seemed warmth in the dog's body. He lifted the head towards his lips. He sniffed under the nose. He could smell no breath. He cupped the head in his hands, his eyes misting over. Then he laid the dog's head down and went to the edge of the water. The mosquitoes swarmed like bees on his head and arms. He didn't care. He wanted to drink.

Then he smelt the smoke. Hundreds of years of instinct learned unconsciously from his ancestors came into play. The smoke was coming from downstream. It was not cooking smoke, not smoke made from a fire with food on it. It was a fire doused with oils to keep away mosquitoes while someone rested or slept.

The smoke led Dan through the trees along the bank of the water as he followed the scent his instinct carried. He might not be a killer but he was a tracker. His hands outstretched to tighten his reflexes, he placed each foot flat and slanted outwards, his knees bent ready to stop at the slightest noise. He followed the wind, with it always in his nostrils, never behind. He breathed only lightly and stayed away from all trees except pines and poplars because their powerful scent overrode all others.

In less than ten minutes he stood, bloody and aching, on the other side of a small clearing.

Propped against a tree, seeming to face him, was Andy. From where Dan stood, in a pool of blackness he saw Andy was awake, but his eyes seemed heavy. He had wrapped a handkerchief around his neck. As if to protect his wounds, his hands wrapped his chest.

Now that he had found the man, Dan began to feel the hunger of revenge in him. The feeling was so close to his nature it started to build itself until it filled his mind with sweet, expectant odours.

He was going to kill this man. And now was the time to do it. It was, he told himself, a matter of simple self-preservation. He raised his hunting knife. He poised it, the pain in his right shoulder was great, but it would not affect his aim. Twenty feet away, Andy moved slightly. Dan was sure that he had not seen him. His fingers tightened on the knife handle. It was coiled ready to leap from his hand.

Dan told himself to let it go. He could not miss. But the knife stayed in his fingers, the handle resting heavy on his palm. A man could do anything if he pressed all his thought into one arrow-sharp point in his mind and gave it all the energy in his body. In this state, Dan let a second pass.

It was too long. The barrel of Andy's rifle snapped up. The muzzle flared. The shot hit the poplar beside Dan's head and in that fraction a whole lifetime went through him. He cursed himself for his schoolbook, church-going white man's thinking.

He threw the knife. It hit Andy on the chest. The man never moved again. It went home clean between the fourth and fifth ribs and buried itself almost to the hilt. Dan's arm relaxed. A surge of pain. His fingers were bleeding. They had caressed the blade. His palm was raw from the force of the butt.

Dan stepped from the side of the tree and took the four paces needed to reach Andy. He was dead, of course, and his rifle rested on his knees. Dan sat beside him looking into his face. It was as if he were alive. Dan got up, took out the knife, stamping out the fire.

Andy was surely dead. There was no doubt about it. The first orange tint of the rising sun hit his body. It was an angry sun, an angry day. Instead of feeling the primeval power of the triumph of his race over an enemy, he felt sick at his first killing.

It was a feeling he was to get many times in the months ahead. He took up one of Andy's huge hands. The warmth of life was still in it, although its fellow members were dead. Dan rubbed it between his own hands as if trying to rub back the life. He held the warm hand for minutes and could imagine the blood still coursing through it. He would remember that warmth for as long as he lived.

He worked until the sun was well up, piling stones over his victim to keep away the wolves and bears. On Tuesday or Wednesday when he reached Fort Norman he would tell the story to Father Binamet. The old priest would keep clear his conscience and stand by him.

When he had finished he walked slowly back to where he had left his small pack of food and belongings. He had killed an enemy. Not so long ago it was the final entrance into warriorship. It was the time for great rejoicing. Now Dan felt sick. If anything, he felt less of a man. The revenge, once won, was sour. There was a lot more he had to learn yet. Things of much greater importance or perhaps one thing of ultimate importance. He would find out.

When he reached his camp site he walked over to the prostrate dog. To his amazement the animal tried to lift its head. Dan fell on his knees and cushioned the head in his lap, the past minutes vanished from his memory, as he sang a song of his people which told of the bravery of the wolf in a battle with the bear and how man and wolf became friends. He sang quietly but the three-note song sounded above the trees and across the river, laden with the emotion of his heart-broken joy.

He stayed with the dog nearly two days and then, in Andy's canoe, the two of them started paddling downstream to Fort Norman.

He had little food and the dog was very ill. It would take him another two days. He kept singing, making up songs with strong stories in them, and very soon the horror of what he had done in the bush was dwarfed by a feeling of fullness inside him, because he and the dog had become one, even as it licked its wounds to heal them. And the fullness was something new and exciting for it was a real love for another, even though it was an animal, a love not unlike what he imagined it would be like with a woman, filled with joy and anxiety at the same moment, tinged with sadness in its ecstasy.

And finally the familiar brought him back to reality. They rounded a bend on the second day and there was Fort Norman, stretched in architectural turpitude along the edge of the Mackenzie River.

THIRTEEN

The settlement of Fort Norman spread along a bank of mud in a two-mile sweep of a bend in the river. It was flat, treeless and almost bare of vegetation of any sort for about a mile inland towards Great Bear Lake. The collection of dilapidated shacks, the large, wooden two-storey building housing the mission boarding school, the primitive, clapboard churches (Catholic green, Anglican grey), the white-fronted Hudson Bay Store, without any steps to the screendoor, with its factor's house attached, all seemed placed on the mud-flat in such a careless way as to have been thrown there from the hand of some giant in a passing canoe.

There was a road. Dirt, deep-rutted and engineered by the half-dozen trucks and other assorted vehicles which plied its mile length. The road had a tributary, snaking back out into the bush, where people went to get wood, to start out on their traplines and to hunt the rabbits, muskrat, partridge and other small edibles which inhabited the bush.

It ended in another group of shacks, abandoned ever since

the old oil drilling had been abandoned and the Oklahoma oil company which had sent a crew up to drill a test hole had gone home.

There were very few houses on the river side of the road. The Bay Store, the cemetery, the new school and the yellow wood of Pfeffer's Place, a hotel, dance hall and place of repute (ill or favoured according to your habits). Behind all this, pulled up across the mud bank were rows of canoes. All colours imaginable, each with its special mounting for the "kicker" or outboard motor, and nearby a stake with a husky chained to it, a guardian remnant of former times.

Father Binamet used to say that there weren't many remnants left and he even bemoaned the fact that Chuck Andrews the settlement chief was planning to have running water added to the two hundred-odd homes. Right now the wooden duck-boards which ran along the side of the road in front of most homes had an inch of rusty piping running the length of it. At intervals there were water taps to which mothers sent their children with buckets. The pipe started out in the river. It ended where the road finished. This served pretty well in summer and caused a lot of neighbourly activity which the old priest liked. In winter drinking water was easier to come by. Children went each morning in their parkas and filled buckets with snow or ice which their mothers melted on the oil stoves in the greasy kitchens of the cabins.

But all of this was home to Dan. And in spite of the fact that he hated much of it, especially the lethargy of the people, it was in his blood in a special way. He thought that most people must hate home in one way or another, relishing only the flavour of its meaning which had etched itself inside them through living there. This flavour came out in such things as the smell of the scrubbed boards of the school, the creosoted scent of the church porch, the heavy perfume of caribou stew on a cold day. It also made itself felt through the texture of a riverside rock, the sights of familiar old, bent figures, of bright children's faces and of old man Nickelsen dead in his coffin frozen stiff at sixty below, outside the Bay Store waiting for spring burial. Dan also thought that none of these things really meant home. They were just the strings which pulled the whole darn thing out from inside people.

But right now Dan was still sitting in the canoe and looking at it all. He had a lot to think about. He could see the settlement, but he doubted if anyone could see him. He had steered the canoe behind the rocks near where the water-pipe entered the river. At this point there were a few scrubby pieces of cover and a deserted cabin.

The float plane came overhead and landed on the mud beach. Must be Jeff Wolgar's Cessna. But even as he thought it, he knew it wasn't. The Cessna was already in, tied to the floating dock. Might be the mail. Might be the Bay supply plane. Might even be someone from Inuvik or Aklavik. What did he care! He first had to decide what to do with the dog. He was still scared they would shoot it. The animal was now so close to him. It had the courage and it deserved to live.

Dan beached the canoe, eventually dragging it with the sick dog in it, through the sparse brush beside the cave. It was cold and very damp inside. The fetid smell of stale urine overpowered him. Nevertheless, he managed to drag the canoe inside and to cover it with some brush.

Then he cupped his arms under the dog, who could not yet find the strength to do more than raise its head to lick its wounds, and he carried the dog out of the cave into the sunlight.

Dan knew of a deserted cabin about a hundred and fifty yards upstream. It took him twenty minutes to reach it, the dog occasionally growling with pain as it lay in his arms.

There wasn't much inside the cabin. A broken table, a chair and a rotting mattress. The door had been torn off and was lying against the wall. Glass from the broken windows splintered under his feet. He put the dog on the mattress.

"Kayuk," he said slowly, repeating, "Kayuk, from now on that is surely your name, my friend." He was hoping for some sign of recognition. But none came. "Sleep! Stay! I'll be back."

He went to the canoe again and took out a can of beef stew which Sam had packed him. Inside the canoe, under the kicker plate, was a bailing can. It was a gallon oil drum cut in half by some enterprising person. He took it to the river and filled it.

Back inside the cabin he opened the can of stew and placed the water on the floor near Kayuk's head. Perhaps the dog would not live through the night. Dan was determined to give him every chance. The dog had the will. Kayuk! He hoped like hell the animal would live and stay his friend. He took the dog's nose in his hands and ran his finger down the snout across the soft fur. "You're a great feller. I'll be back. Don't move now." The animal seemed conscious enough to understand, but no sign came from the long drooping tail.

He placed the broken door across the entrance and propped the chair against it. His last look at the dog made him think the animal was trying to raise its head again. But it was merely a hopeful illusion. Dan turned on his heel, picked up his pack from the canoe and headed for town. He didn't want to delay getting to the Bay store. He hoped to get there before news arrived from Yellowknife.

FOURTEEN

As he began to walk into town, Dan Nelson knew the news was already there. There was nothing unusual visible. No one peered from a corner of a window. There wasn't a collection of people outside Pfeffer's. The Bay Store looked empty, the Catholic church closed. Just a few people, all of whom he knew facially, going about their business. But the air was electric.

Dan closed the door of the Bay Store behind him and looked around him. He smelt stale vegetables and bread which had started life two weeks ago in some bakery in Yellowknife and been barged down river. The short aisles, a copy in miniature of a southern supermarket, was empty of human presence. He took a quick walk down to the long aluminium freezer at the back to make sure that Jim Fawcett the assistant factor or old Mrs Manger, the factor's wife, weren't stocking up from the lean-to which served as a warehouse. No one was there either.

As he came back, he heard voices in the back office, which in times past had been the place where furs were traded. He distinctly heard Bill Manger's voice. Then Father Binamet's. And lastly several other voices. His knuckles hardened on the doorknob. And before he realised it, Manger's voice said, "Come on in."

Dan found himself looking down at the comfortable bulge in Manger's waistline. Manger had risen to open the door. He was a very large, ugly Englishman, with a rare twist of a smile, badly fitting teeth, a head flaking with dandruff and feet covered in carpet slippers. Beside Manger sat Father Binamet, his beard yellowed round the mouth, his gaunt neck with the ancient scar from a fight with a trapper still visible, and his eyes, showing a cold blue glint which as a child scared Dan so much.

Seated behind him was Ted Ziegel.

Dan heard him say, "Well, now we were just talking about you, lad. Bet you didn't expect me here? Came up this morning with Rod and Cunard just to make sure that Bill here gives you everything you need and that he charges it up to me! Can't do too much to help young people in the North get on, can we, Bill?"

Father Binamet rose and put his arm on Dan's shoulder. He stood six foot seven, 72 years old. From the look on his face Dan saw that the old man was telling him to keep his mouth shut. He was in a den of thieves.

"Glad you are back, Dan," the priest said. "I'm afraid it's already all over town. You're a pretty big guy now. I'll be in my study."

The priest lumbered to the door without so much as a smile, nor did he turn to say good-bye to the other two men. When Father Binamet left the room, Dan always felt as if half the room had left. Today it was especially true.

"Now, Dan, sit down and have a chat. I was just telling Bill how we can work this out together . . ." said Ziegel.

Dan stood by the door. He cursed himself for coming. Sure as he was standing there breathing, Ted Ziegel had worked out not only one way, but one way with several alternate plans, to rob him of the gold, his only possession except Kayuk and, in his youthful ignorance, the gateway to the freedom of his family and his Fort Norman people. Ted Ziegel had only to claim that he had found the cave first to enable him to grab nearly all of the money to be made in the mine. It wasn't conjecture. It was the law. Dan Nelson knew it. And Dan Nelson also knew that his youthful foolishness had probably blown the gold straight into Ziegel's hands. The only trick Ziegel had to win was to find where it was, to stake before Dan did and to rush to Yellowknife to register his staking.

"C'mon, Dan boy, sit down. Beer?" Ziegel continued. "Bill, get the guy a beer. Been in a fight or something? You're all cut about."

The remark unnerved Dan. The thought of the killing in the bush had grown in nightmare proportions since he had left the body under the pile of stones. His courage and determination had withered with every step he took away from the scene, and in their place a series of guilt-ridden thoughts had etched themselves into his head.

And yet the killing was not all black. The call of his ancestors was strong also. This call was towards the justice of man in the natural law although tinged with revenge as it was with Dan, it did not change the facts.

But right now, he was tired, weak and scared.

"Now, is that any better, lad?" said Ziegel as Dan sipped the beer.

As Ziegel's voice droned on it suddenly struck Dan why he was more openly interested. Ziegel had the full assay from Ottawa now. It must have arrived after Dan left Yellowknife. The thought, even in his confused state, brought a smile to Dan. He must be on to something very big indeed for Ziegel's interest to have increased so much with the assay report.

Dan sipped the beer and almost immediately went to the sink and vomited. Ziegel said, "Go home, get some rest and come and meet with us all here tonight. You'll feel better then."

Without saying another word, Dan rose and unsteadily made his way to the door. Ziegel's voice was in his ear and his sweaty arm on his shoulder. The words he was saying were just that—words. They had no meaning to Dan.

He heard them as he walked down the street to the rectory. People stopped to talk to him. Some shook his hand, but he didn't even recognise their faces. All was a blur.

He passed his own home. His mother would probably be in the back cooking. But he did not stop.

Father Binamet's study was just off the hall, to the right. Dan knew every nook and cranny. He had come three nights a week, when other boys were out playing hockey, to study. He and his elder brother were star pupils that the old priest saw as growing out of the morass that was their lot in the Arctic to see the world in a larger light and to give more to it. They were both university class and exceptionally courageous and bright like many from the Mackenzie Valley. His younger brother, David, a cripple from polio, was the same. Binamet had come north to the mission thirty years ago to find a life. He had found it. He was hoping to send the three brothers into the world, also to find a life.

Dan found the study door open and the old man behind his desk. He walked in without knocking and sat in his usual chair on the other side of the stove. The room smelt of books and dampness. Indeed it was so filled with anachronistic books of almost every description that the priest seemed to be sitting in a hole in the middle of a room of books.

"So you are here? Some tea? You have been in a fight or two?"

"It's nothing. How are you?"

"The weather is good and my sciatica is much better."

"I'm glad. Well, I'm in trouble . . ."

"I know. I told you it is a horrible game. It is a disease. Men and gold are cancerous."

"I am not in trouble about the gold, Father."

"No? I think you may be. But no matter. What do you want of me?"

"I want to go to confession."

There was a pause and then the priest said, "Yes. We will go into the church . . ."

"I can confess here. As we used to when . . ."

The old man laughed. "As you used to when you last went as a boy?"

Dan laughed back. "Yes, Father."

"Very well. Kneel, Daniel Nelson."

By the time, several minutes later, that Dan had finished telling the priest the story, he was weeping again. This time it was in relief.

The old priest sat back. "You know, don't you, that I cannot give you absolution."

"I expected you to say that."

"But I will give you absolution if you go to the authorities, for I know you are not guilty, and even if you were and were penitent, I would absolve you. God would do his justice."

There was another pause. Dan could hear his own heart. The old man's hand came out and placed itself over Dan's. The fingers were like long gnarled bones, but strong and strangely warm. They reminded Dan of Andy's.

Dan said, "I will go to the police, Father."

"Yes. We will go together." He looked into Dan's face. "You can sleep here in the spare room. It will be better. Out there," he tilted his head to indicate the street, "there will be a lot going on and there will be trouble. Now let me get you tea and some food. Both Isabella and Maria Teresa laid this morning, so I shall make you an omelette. Is it not silly an old priest talking about two hens as if they were human? I am too old."

"Why don't you go back to Belgium?" asked Dan.

"Thirty years is a long time," the priest said with a slight smile, "and besides—are you so ready to be rid of me?"

After eating the meal the old man cooked for him, Dan fell into the bed in the visitor's room and was asleep almost before the priest closed the door.

FIFTEEN

That night Dan went to see Kayuk, with food from the old priest. The dog seemed to know him, but Dan thought it might just be his imagination. He came back the next day, and on the third day the dog was much better, recognising Dan's approach and greeting it with a grumbling bark. The wound in his side, which the animal had kept assiduously clear of flies, was not crusted over and although the ribs were obviously broken, the dog could not rest on its stomach as well as on its side. The right back leg wound was clean. The bullet had not touched the bone as far as Dan could tell. The hole was healing with a small ring of burnt flesh around it.

Each day Dan made the dog as comfortable as he could, even feeding him with a spoon. Dan's heart was lighter whenever he saw Kayuk and he would sing to him about his happiness.

After he had seen Kayuk on the third day, he went with the priest to the federal building in town, a small shack which contained the post office, the telephone and unemployment and welfare offices. The priest telephoned the RCMP in Yellowknife and Dan never even spoke.

After that the priest told him to go to his mother. She was worried.

The cabin was musty and the heat (for it was now late August) was unbearable. But the old woman, always chilled, wore a shawl on her shoulders and had two naked grandchildren at her feet. She was a tough, lean woman, aged and yet ageless, who had ten children, Dan being the second. She acted as if he had never left town, and pretended that she didn't know. But sitting at her kitchen table while she made tea and slapped the backsides of the fighting grandchildren, Dan told her everything, speaking in Cree, which is a sing-song language of great emotional range to those who are born to it. Her face hardly showed what she felt and she never spoke until the story was told. Then she sat down with a sigh and lifted her wrinkled face to his. "Give up the gold."

"No." During the last few days his heart had hardened into a fierce desire for it. And the pain he was feeling at what had happened was burned into determination—a consuming fire which had not existed like this before it had been kindled by the reactions of other men.

"No!" he repeated. "I have gone so far that I cannot now turn back. It is necessary to finish it."

"Thomas will be coming home again at Christmas. Leave this idea aside and go with him to California. Make a life outside together. There is no more life for you here. We are the last generation who will make a home here. This place is no good. Look at me. Go. Your brothers and sisters have gone. Don't stay here. This place is finished." Sullenly she sipped her tea from the saucer as he had always seen her do. She looked so old, yet she could not be more than 60. She put the saucer down and went on, "When your father and I first came here from Great Bear, the river was running fast and the fish were good. Plenty of lake trout. There was elk and caribou in the mountains. Lots of ducks. But most of those animals have moved away, even most of the fish. No, this place is not for us. I shall only stay here to die."

Dan said nothing for a while.

He eventually said, "Mother, you are right. But I shall not go. Even with the gold, and lots of money in the bank in some place in the South, I'll stay. There are others, young people, who are like me."

"Not many, Dan. Go. If you can get out. Go."

"No. I shall not," he said.

And he went on to tell her about Sam, the girl he had met in Yellowknife, for somehow the train of conversation seemed to lead naturally that way. And she nodded her old head and rubbed the heads of both her grandchildren, her face empty of thoughts and her eyes closed . . .

"I'm tired. Can you find their mother?" she said absently.

"I think she's in the store."

Dan got up and took out his wallet. The priest had given him ten dollars. He placed the bill on the table and turned to the door. "I'll be seeing you. I'll find Jeanette and tell her to collect them."

He never turned to watch the old woman's eyes on his back as he left. She was glad he didn't. She was filled with fear. She ached with it, not a healthy fear like before birth, but a salty sickness.

Dan, in the August sun again, was thinking about the girl, Sam, but he made his way back to the priest's house.

The next day, the fourth day of his return, he went early to see Kayuk and was pleasantly surprised to see him standing on the end of the mattress, playfully tearing at the flocking. The dog hobbled towards him without putting much weight on the healing back leg.

"Well, you are a fine one. A real fine guy," Dan said, kneeling and pressing the dog's muzzle to his ear. "Why don't you tell me how proud you are? You're a proud bugger. And with reason!"

Dan started to laugh and to pat the dog on the back, while it licked his ear and under his chin where the salty perspiration trickled.

"You dog! You are not like other dogs. Look at you." Dan reached out and pulled up the tail trying to make it curve up instead of drooping and brushing the floor. "Why can't you make your tail stand up like any decent animal?" Dan laughed again and began to play with the dog as if it were a puppy, having it hobble after odd stones and pieces of wood in the room, his thoughts happily settling to the thought that the dog was mending quickly. As the morning went on, he chained Kayuk with the length of chain he had brought with him to the door post of the old cabin, and walked down to the river's edge, thinking other thoughts.

Why did Sam's face keep appearing in his mind? Was she trying to tell him something? What had made him tell his mother about her? There would now be gossip around the town. He made his way back, even more determined to stay away from everyone except the priest, who seemed content to have him at the rectory. A lot was going to happen in the next few days. It was not going to be pleasant and he wished many times that he could just run away into the bush and wait it out. For ever, if it took that long. It took all the will-power he had to stay, and it was crazy things like the dog and Sam's face that made him always decide to see it all through.

On the morning of the fifth day, the dog was even better. He was growing fat on the chain and Dan wanted to let him have a run but he dared not do it. While he was playing with the animal at the cabin two aircraft went over and landed on the water. One was a twin-engined Otter, and Dan saw a lot of people get off. The other was Larry Gibbs's Beaver plane from Yellowknife and people with cameras and radio equipment got off and went into Pfeffer's place.

Dan made his way back to the rectory via the backs of the houses. From his window upstairs he looked out behind the fly-blown net curtaining, on the growing scene in the street below. A great many people came to Fort Norman that day.

Lawyers, newspapermen, radio and television people. They walked quickly, swatting at the mosquitoes—talking to almost anyone. But they never came to see Dan, who had apparently become quite a celebrity. Some of the people came from as far away as Vancouver and Toronto. The old priest hid the radio and burnt the newspapers so that Dan would not see them and do something rash, like run away. The murder had caught on in the dreary vacation news of August. It had a macabre quality, and they called it a ritual killing in the bush. There were many murders and other serious crimes every year in the Arctic, but it so happened that this one got the full play.

Later that day another plane load of people arrived. They were officials, some from Ottawa, some from Yellowknife. It was not just because these people were not of Dan's race that he disliked them. It was not because they wore strange blue suits, unsuitable polished shoes and carried great leather brief-cases. It was not even that they behaved strangely to the people in the town. They were different. Odd. Oddities. But Dan disliked them because of the way they looked on him, a Cree. There were four centuries of anger in Dan, four centuries in which unsuitably dressed people had intruded on the life of his people and plundered, robbed, raped and starved them into submission, which these strangers even today took to be peace. Rage and terror was what Dan felt when he saw their collars and ties, their shining pink faces. Their shouting and hearty scuffling around Pfeffer's place produced a music in his ears. It was the music of the enemy. A pounding music swelling in him. The swelling of the sweetness of revenge.

They rigged up a court in the dance hall at Pfeffer's place and half of the town came to see as Dan was led in to face the magistrate. The Mounties were there in force. One asked him if he needed an interpreter! The same man, a sergeant, then said he would be charging him. How could the man interpret fairly for him and charge him at the same time? Anyway Dan said no. Father Binamet was representing him. The priest sometimes did this as part of his duties. He spoke perfect Cree and he knew the law, even tribal law.

Before the sun went behind the mountains on the other side of the river, Dan had been bound over under the surveillance of Father Binamet, charged with wilful murder and booked to appear at the next sitting of the assize sessions at the court's convenience. It all took a few minutes to pronounce and before it was dark all the court officials, including the police, had left by plane again. Only the newspapermen stayed, they waited for a picture of the ritual murderer of the Arctic. They waited and waited.

So did Ted Ziegel, Rod and Cunard. Dan spotted them from his window before the priest called him down to supper. Dan was lucky to be left with the priest, whose pleas stopped the police taking him to the jail in Yellowknife to await trial. But he knew now that he could not go after the gold until it was all over. Andy was dead. His death was a law of nature. At times you had to kill to protect your own life. But Dan knew they would put him in jail if they could. The anger inside him grew like a baby inside a woman.

Dan went to bed and dreamed that the dog died and that Sam had married someone else. He woke wondering what she was thinking of the news, which he now knew had been broadcast across the whole country. It was not just. There was no justice. It made him all the more determined to carry out his plans about the gold. The whole thing was designed in his mind to teach them a lesson. All of them, but especially Ziegel, who in his greed had fallen into a trap.

SIXTEEN

Life in an isolated settlement has a short memory for things which get in the way of its inner rhythms, and Dan's arrest and detention were to Fort Norman, like other foreign intrusions, soon a mere piece of background gossip.

The old priest occasionally accompanied him for an evening stroll along the river or to the Bay Store, where Rod and Cunard waited impatiently, almost constantly playing cards or drinking with Bill Manger. Otherwise, Dan moved fairly freely, keeping away from anyone who expressed even the vaguest interest in questioning him. The days were hot. The air was as stifling as the pressure of the waiting.

It was said by some that the next assize sessions of the court of the Northwest Territories would be in September. Others shook their heads and said they had known the authorities often took much longer than that. Dan might just as well expect to be under supervision for a year or more.

In other words, the settlement went about its business but kept one eye open wondering if Dan might bring another burst of excitement by running away into the bush or whether, after trial and surely a successful plea of self-defence, he would then set out to stake his claim.

The fever was still there. It had spread underground and smouldered under the roots of the tiny community. Asleep, yes, but with one eye open and roving.

Three days after Dan Nelson was arrested and charged, the remaining four members of the Canadian press corps had disappeared aboard a Pacific Western Airlines flight bound for Edmonton. That same day, Kayuk placed his foot on the ground and put weight on it.

He hobbled at the end of the chain for nearly a mile upstream to one of those unexpected encounters in the Arctic landscape. There were a number of permanent hot springs around, especially in the Nahanni Valley, but this particular patch of green nestled under small pines and Arctic spruce beside the river. Here the man-boy and the wolf-dog spent several hours in complete isolation and happiness watching the bubbling hot water. The bond between them was now very great.

And Andy, now buried decently under Mackenzie mud, near where he was killed, his body marked by a crude wooden cross which would soon rot as the material which it marked was to rot, was almost forgotten by most at Fort Norman. But no man's spirit dies with him and so it was passed on to others in the settlement, enkindling the same flames of greed.

Dan wished almost daily that he could contact Sam in Yellowknife. She strayed into his thoughts so often, but he needed new confidence to write or to phone. Often in the small iron bed in the old priest's house, he would go to sleep determined to call her the following day. Yet he always found an excuse to put off the call.

He had begun many a letter, only to crumple it and toss it away. What had he to say to her anyway? There was nothing between them. Nothing to recall. And, as far as he knew, nothing to hope for now.

She would have heard his news. It seemed everyone had. She probably didn't give it all much more thought. Yet he somehow could not imagine her believing half the stories now circulating. Perhaps she would not even want to hear any more about him. That was quite possible and he made himself try to forget her too. But it didn't work easily, although it drove him closer to the one other strong element in his life—the dog Kayuk. Kayuk was the one element, also, which he was sure he still had in common with Sam.

SEVENTEEN

Had he known it, Sam was feeling much the same as Dan, self-conscious, worried and lonely.

The café never fully occupied Sam for more than a few hours a day. Nearly all her customers came with the shift changes at the mine. And even when they were in, the work was so routine that she could not stop her mind roaming as she worked.

The news of Dan's arrest had come to her via Bill Godfrey, the *News of the North*'s reporter, who happened to come in for a coffee on his way to do a story. Minutes later it was on the radio and within the living organism of the town was passed into the gossip circuit by supper time.

Sam's first reaction to it was controlled disbelief. And after that complete panic. She had tried to phone Fort Norman, over three hundred miles north across the wasteland, but she never got through, although once the old priest had been called to the primitive phone in the government offices and he had re-assured her. She doubted if he had told Dan, but she had left a message to call or write. Distances are painful in the Arctic and they often seem unable to be bridged. Sam had, it was most evident to her, grown very fond of Dan in the short time she had known him. She wondered if "fond" was the right word? Close? Understanding? Any way she looked at it, she could not see Dan committing murder.

After the realisation settled inside her, she felt miserable, desperate and frustrated. Then, twice again, she tried to phone Dan. On the second try she heard the Fort Norman operator's voice saying she would try to find him. She had written, and subsequently torn up two letters. And then things happened which took her mind off Dan, temporarily.

First, her young cousin Sherry arrived from Saskatoon with a determination never to go "out" again. She had just got fired from her job as receptionist at a motel after a disagreement with the manager's wife regarding her relationship with the manager. In spite of the light-hearted, flippant aura she exuded with her bleached hair and stiletto heels, she was a genuinely pleasant girl with a passion for cooking, cleaning and eating.

"You just leave those bastards to me, Sam," she said about the miners. "Respect! That's what keeps 'em in line. Just give me my food and a bed."

Sam said, "If you want to sleep on the old couch in my room, you are most welcome. Starting today, I could do with some help," she lied.

"Well, you look as if you could do with a rest," Sherry said. "I haven't seen you eat enough to keep a fly since I came. You are too uptight. What's the matter?"

"I'm waiting for my period. Never did have much appetite for anything I cooked anyway," said Sam.

"Well, until the period comes," said Sherry breezily, "you take it easy. How about me cooking you up some supper? What have you got to cook in this café?" she went on, cleaning invisible spots off the counter with a damp cloth.

Sam went outside and lit a cigarette. She was irritated with

Sherry because she was right.

She had never been this late before. She tried to isolate the fact. Was it really happening to her? It was so different when it was you. When it happened to someone else, you felt sorry but you went about your business. You were able to put the idea on one side. But when it was your trouble, inside you, the thought invaded your day, never leaving you.

If she was pregnant, it made her doubly furious that it must be Cunard's child. She detested herself since Cunard left. She had been determined to plunge the bread knife into him whenever she next saw him. But he had disappeared the same day Dan left. Suppose she *was* pregnant? Of course, the thing inside her could not live. Having Cunard's baby was a total impossibility. The mere thought revolted her. It wasn't the baby itself, because it would probably grow up just like any other. It was the thought that someone like Cunard was actually part of her. In the deepest way their bodies had mingled inside to form this—whatever it was that was stopping her period. She wanted to refuse it. To expel the thing. But someone would have to do that for her. The thing had to be taken away.

From when she was a small girl she always let her imagination play on some of the dreadful things that could happen to her. The death of her parents, her being run over by a truck or the sight of a terrible accident at the mine. The act of imagining these things became a lesson in the preparation for their possible advent. And at an imagined missing period she saw herself panicking, wounded, ashamed, hysterical. Now, though, with it actually happening to her, she was merely bitter by being stuck with part of Cunard blocking her insides and usurping her natural functions. Goddam it all!

Sam went inside, throwing away the already extinguished stub of her cigarette. Maybe Sherry was right. She needed a break. Perhaps she could somehow get away to Fort Norman. News around town was that Dan was free, under the supervision of the priest.

The cost of the scheduled flight to Fort Norman was about two hundred and forty dollars, return. She simply hadn't got it. There were people she could borrow from, but right now, with the strong possibility of having to arrange a miscarriage, she didn't want to start borrowing. Of course, if she waited another week it might be possible that she wasn't pregnant at all. Then, as things worked out, she heard one evening that Jeff Wolgar was making a bush flight into Fort Norman on the following Sunday, with three new huge chain-saws for the loggers in the bush at Great Bear Lake. She could see his Cessna float plane, moored to the little dock in the bay below her cabin. Perhaps Jeff would let her hitch in and out. She would beg him for it. He was a nice guy.

EIGHTEEN

Dan's first sight of Sam when she arrived that Sunday was of her carrying a huge bag off the ramp beside the floating Cessna. She was dressed in a dark blue blouse and jeans, white shoes and a brilliant crimson scarf about her neck. Her hair was loose and even in the short weeks he'd been away from her he had forgotten how silky and thick it was. His instinct had been to run to her. But the sight of her seemed to momentarily paralyse him. Instead she threw her arms around him and let the heavy bag slide to the ground between them.

Her lips were eager. They passed over to him a sort of cold heat. And he had been scared that things might have changed!

"I got your telegram," he said.

"I suppose you did."

"Otherwise I wouldn't be here to meet you," he laughed.

They stood apart and looked at each other, embarrassed.

"I brought a picnic. It's such a nice day," she said.

He started to walk her up the road to the rectory of the

Catholic church to meet Father Binamet. But then he changed his mind.

"Well, we'd better go some place private to eat."

"Yes. Jeff Wolgar's flying back at five. I thought it might save time."

"At five! Oh, Sam! Can't you stay? Mum will put you up. I've a lot to tell you."

"We'll make the best of it. I've no other way to get back."

"Can't you get Jeff to take off later? Tomorrow perhaps?" Dan was now walking her to the southern end of town.

Life didn't change much because it was Sunday in Fort Norman. Of course, it was a church day, but after that people went about their business much as usual. Right now few people were about because it was high noon. In summer lunch was a big meal and although some of the children were still out on the duck-boards skipping and playing hop-scotch, most of their parents were already at table.

As they walked, arm in arm, Sam still carrying the bag, Dan told her his side of the story. It was nothing new to her, for she had known all along that Dan was in the right. But it was good to hear him say it. However, it also kindled a nagging worry which was to stay with her for many months.

It was only the beginning. She knew his eventual trial would be a formality, a perfunctory rite. There was little chance of anyone's convicting him. But the gold was something else.

"I'm still going after it, you know," he said.

"I thought you might. But you'll get someone in with you now. You won't go alone?"

"When the snow comes, I'll pick a time," he said.

"Let's talk of something else," she said. "There's ham, potato salad and beer in this," she added, touching the bag.

"It must be heavy then," he said, taking it.

"Take me some place where we can sit peacefully."

"And you can dream?"

"Nothing wrong with dreaming. But I want to talk."

She had brought her personal worry with her. Should she

tell him her news? She didn't want to spoil the day and she still was not sure she was pregnant. Also she was frightened that he would not want to have anything to do with her afterwards. She had worried a lot about that and coming down river in the plane she remembered that Cunard was said to be in Fort Norman with Rod, on a job for his father. If Dan knew he would probably kill him and this time he'd have no defence. So she kept silent, trying to let a decision seep to the surface on its own.

They walked in silence through the last few houses of the settlement and the path, then went along the river bank, a sandy bed for their feet.

"It's not far," he said, after half a mile. Both were much more relaxed and happy, her head came onto his shoulder, he slowed his pace to stay in step with hers.

"I missed you," she said.

"I began to wonder if I'd ever see you again."

"I tried to get to you, but somehow never made it."

"I thought maybe the news had driven you away—did it?"

"From the first, I knew. I said that's not Dan. Dan couldn't do that without a reason."

They had turned a bend in the river and the path veered left into the bush. Dan took her arm and led her through some trees to the back of a run-down, empty cabin.

"Look," he said, pointing at the window. Kayuk stood with his paws on the sill and the chain wrapped round his ear.

"Kayuk!" she yelled. "You've still got the dog! That's a surprise. I'm so glad."

She ran forward and pushed the dog's nose under her arm hugging him and at the same time trying to release the chain from his head. "Oh, you stupid old thing. You beautiful, big, crazy animal."

Dan reached up and undid the chain and the dog immediately bounced forward at them with great force, wagging itself at Sam and crouching under the palm of her hand like a young puppy. "You big baby. You baby!" she cried.

Dan calmed Kayuk down and then they carried their lunch further through the bush on a track which Kayuk knew well for he bounded ahead.

The hot spring was reached with only a few more minutes' walking. The sight of it overwhelmed Sam. She'd never seen anything like it.

"It's a fairlyland. I'd never have believed it," she shouted, dancing away from him and running up the rocks to feel the warm, soft water bubbling up through the granite.

The hot spring forced itself out of the rock face into a pool some twenty feet above the river and tumbled over rocks, worn smooth by the passage of water into the stream which led to a larger pool where the cold river water mixed with the hot and made a superb bathing place.

"There's a current but it's OK. You can swim," Dan said, tying Kayuk under a tree beside the water.

Now she stood, the hot water splashing round her feet as she looked on in childish wonderment. There was a grove of small study poplar to her left and under it stood clumps of golden rod, wild iris and sweet-williams. The tall grass, something Sam had never seen in the North, was like a hay meadow around the grove, and on a sandy slope towards the river's bank was a profusion of wild primulas, violas and peonies.

"D'you like it?" he said, smiling.

"It's fabulous! Truly beautiful," she said.

"When we first came to live here, there used to be a cabin set right there," he said, pointing to the knee-length grass. "An old English lady who had come out here as a prospector years ago lived in it."

"And she planted the garden?"

"It got out of hand a bit. But you see those trees on the other side of the pool? They say some of them are maples. I wouldn't know because I've never seen a maple. The old lady used to keep a cow here and ride into Fort Norman on a donkey."

"And in winter? What happens to the hot spring in winter?"

"Just this little area is free of snow. I've swum here when the ice was seven foot thick on the river."

"It's a paradise, Dan."

"One day, I'm going to get this water piped into the settlement."

She undid the top button on her jeans, and let them slip to the rock. "Coming in?"

"Perhaps. We'll put the food in the shade," he said, taking it to the tree under which Kayuk was lying pretending to sleep.

When he looked up again she was swimming naked in the warm pool, the white of her arm in brilliant contrast to the blackness of her hair. Her body had a rhythm in tune to the water. It seemed to slip effortlessly through it. Her long legs kicking in a lazy, relaxed beat. "Join me! Come on!" she shouted.

"Can't make up my mind."

She turned on her back in the water. He was still a shy boy. Seeing her on her back, her long hair trembling over her shoulders past the brown pointed nipples and the flat white of her stomach with the black triangle of hair between her legs, made him more shy. Of course, he would join her! He'd thought of it every time he'd come here with Kayuk. But it still took guts to strip off in front of her.

He joined her, hurriedly, at first swimming around the pool quickly, savouring the water, sniffing the faint sulphurous smell and afterwards locked behind her as they swam together, his arm round the hardness of her breasts and the firmness of her buttocks against his stomach. His shyness began to wane, and he was filled with the thought of having her in his arms.

She said, "I'm hungry."

"Yes," he said, "I'm hungry too."

They climbed out and shook off the water, like dogs. She started to unzip the lunch pack. But she stopped as he caught her hand and pulled her to him. He could hold back no longer.

"Come on," he said, kissing her firmly.

"I thought you said you were hungry!" she managed at the end of the first long kiss. But after that she relaxed against him.

"OK, then come and lie down beside me," said Sam, glad he had made the move.

She spread her clothes under her to pillow herself on the rock.

Dan stood waiting, half wondering what he should do.

"Come on," she said. "Oh, Dan!" she laughed. "Kneel beside me." He slipped to his knees, the tall grass on either side of the rocks forming a natural curtain. He ran his left hand up over her thighs and along her stomach. He felt her nipples stiffen.

He closed his eyes. When all thought becomes one thought, and when all emotion becomes one emotion, it is like being God, he said to himself.

He eased himself on top of her and gave his total consciousness to her body. Once he remembered hearing Kayuk yawn. But mostly he heard the squeak of their wet bodies as he finally pushed down and into the warm, dark tunnel that was the inside of her.

Over his shoulder, Sam occasionally saw a glimpse of rays of sun through the poplar and the tall grass. She thought, "Now, is this really happening to me?" The excitement of Dan's body and the joy of being with him surpassed everything. As her insides were drawn together in one final burst of joy, she felt Dan also climax.

Was there any other joy like it? Was giving birth a greater joy? Was it Dan himself or what he represented on top of her which made her feel differently? For she did feel different. Her body had changed. Her fingers were not as they had been before, as they ran themselves gently over Dan's back, they were someone else's fingers, and someone else's feet were under his. As he pulled slowly out of her and turned on his side on the warm rock, she wondered if he too felt the same. Did he have his fingers and she his? Was his body able to wash away the body Cunard had left in her? The thought angered her and disturbed her peace.

"*Now*, I'm hungry," he said.

"Hungry? Yes. I am too. But first I'm going to cool off," she said, jumping once more into the pool. He watched her swim slowly in circles.

She was thinking she could obliterate the Cunard in her. It would happen that way. She was suddenly glad she had not told Dan. Now was not the time. When she joined him he had not moved.

"Was it all right, Sam?"

"It was perfect."

"You were scowling when you jumped in the pool."

"You know me and my moods. I always do when I'm thinking. Let's eat." She began to lay out the lunch.

During lunch she kept the smile on her face, but her mind was like an engine on an old train, puffing along trying to make a hill. Was it conscience which pricked her to tell him? Or was it damn foolishness? Would she ever know? She reached her still wet hand into her jeans pocket while Dan still ate. She needed a cigarette and she would be all right. She dragged the smoke down inside her lungs, through a mouth still tasting of fresh bread, tomatoes, cheese and beer. He leaned forward towards her.

There was a pause and then he said, "Sam—there's something I should tell you about Andy."

"You wanted to kill him?"

"No, he was trying to get *me* all right. He fired first. No. It's that I was not sorry about it. I'm not now."

"Did you get a kick out of it?"

"No. I felt sick. I still feel sick."

"Why, now?" she asked.

"Because of you. I was thinking of you."

"In what way?"

"What you'd think about me. Worrying that you might not understand."

She took his arm and drew him to her, his head resting on her breasts and her hand stroking his temple.

He finally said, "It's good now. It's really very good. I mean

I'm sure, thank God." Kayuk gave another yawn.

Sam said, "I guess he's telling us something."

"Do you approve, Kayuk, you big ugly bastard?"

The dog looked at her, his head on one side and ears up. His tail was sweeping the shade in which he lay.

Suddenly Sam repeated, "Dan, don't go after the gold."

"As soon as the snow falls, I will go after it. I will be ready," he added.

They dressed and walked back to the dock where Jeff Wolgar was waiting with his Cessna. There, as they said good-bye, she asked the question again. But he didn't answer, so she said, "If you go, I'll come along with you." It drew a distant smile from Dan.

As the plane took off and she saw him standing there, unmoving, unwaving, she thought it had been a good day and a happy time. She would come back after she had rid herself of the thing inside her.

Dan went back to the rectory and happily ate supper in silent peace, facing Father Binamet, whose hooded eyes also read his thoughts. It had been a day of days for Dan. The priest was pleased.

NINETEEN

Towards the end of September when the air was filled with bitter wind and the waters lay like heavy oil on the lakes signifying impending ice, Dan Nelson was summoned to appear at the assize sessions in Fort Smith to stand trial and Samantha had her prayers answered and obtained a renewed courage.

Doctors took her into the small, bright hospital at Yellowknife and removed a benign cyst from her uterus, and her periods started again immediately. The pregnancy was a phantom. Two days later she was out of hospital and making plans to try to join Dan at his trial.

The RCMP came for Dan. Two of them arrived at the front door of the rectory. There wasn't anyone on the streets, but there wasn't a soul who didn't know. One of the RCMP officers handed a warrant to Father Binamet who was acting as Dan's counsel.

The custom was to engage an RCMP officer to defend a man. The system was filled with injustice to the old priest, because the police also acted as crown attorneys. The result too was that most people just pleaded guilty, went to jail for a month and left to commit the same crimes again. The handing of the warrant to the priest was a typical example of bureaucratic slight. The constable knew that Dan could read, but custom still dictated the tradition that few Indians could.

The four men marched down the street, Dan handcuffed on either side of the two policemen, and Father Binamet striding behind, a half-head taller than either officer.

As they reached the end of the small dock where the plane was tethered, the constable to Dan's left undid the handcuff and for the first time Dan had the urge to break and run.

But he caught the eye of the priest. Dan put his left hand on the warm aluminium door and he pulled himself inside the Otter.

He could feel the sweat breaking out on his neck. What if things went wrong and his plea of self-defence was rejected? Could he live through ten years cooped up like an animal in a cage? The RCMP Otter circled the town and Dan could see that people were coming out into the street. The other constable undid the other handcuff and lit a cigarette. He offered one to the priest but not to Dan. Dan took one of his own, rolling it between his fingers and trying hard to push away his fear.

A panic in his throat made him swallow and then cough. They said that a lot of people jailed at Fort Smith killed themselves. Would it be possible to escape? Even if he waited for his term to end, how would he be after he got out—he had talked to many natives who had been in jail. They usually went back.

Come on, Dan! You haven't been tried yet! Everyone is saying you'll get off. The trial is routine, an obstacle, not the end! You are weak to be thinking that way. Sam would tell you that.

Sam? How would it be with Sam if he went to jail? It would be the end of all that, he supposed. What in hell's name had driven him to kill the guy?

As if in answer to his self-questioning the priest's hand came over his. The priest said, "Don't worry, I shall do everything I can."

Cold words.

"There is a dog," Dan began suddenly. "I've been hiding him. He followed me all the way from Yellowknife. A stray. Part wolf." He paused. The old priest's eyes were on the bouncing floor of the aircraft, a habit when someone started to confess. Dan went went on, "He saved my life when Andy first attacked."

"Why didn't you say that before?"

"You'd have had to kill the dog."

"Where is he now, Dan?" the priest whispered.

"In the shed at the back of Mum's. Dave, my brother, has promised to feed him in the bush. Don't let them shoot him."

There was a pause. The old priest seemed to be praying.

"You will do as I say, Father?"

"Yes. But you should have told me. It may make a difference. It will be better for you. A dog needs some provocation to attack."

The plane landed at Fort Smith where a police van with bars on the back waited. Dan was bundled into it and within minutes booked into the jail, where he shared a cell with eleven other people awaiting trial. The cell was surprisingly clean, smelling like a hospital. But it was small, originally made for four people. The others already knew he was coming. They did not speak to Dan, except to make way for him to sit on the floor of the almost furnitureless place. It was not that they were scared of Dan, even though they knew he was up for murder. They were afraid of almost everything.

Dan had not been there more than half an hour when he already knew that living in a cell was something he could not do. It seemed to him the most devilish device man had ever invented and that death was preferable. He also learned in that short time what it's like to be a trapped animal.

Meanwhile, Father Binamet was met by his bishop's secretary. The bishop had an office in Fort Smith. They did not discuss the case, but that afternoon Father Binamet paid a visit to the court and talked at length to the judge.

The next morning, Dan had to wait until all other cases were heard before he was handcuffed and led to the dock.

The judge came in and all stood. Flanked by two Mounties in scarlet and under a picture of the Queen, the young judge sat and the court was called to order.

Dan caught a smile from Father Binamet. The Mountie representing the case for the Crown was from Ottawa. He was a fully trained lawyer as well as a policeman. He was in plain clothes.

The case did not last long. Dan felt dizzy and hot. He tried to listen to what was going on, but his mind went into fantasy. He imagined himself away from the courtroom, and involved himself in a long story about Sam and Kayuk. It was a dream. And, because of the horror of his surroundings, it was more real than his present life.

When he was called to the stand by the priest he answered each question almost as if it were delivered in isolation.

Whether it was an hour later or three, Dan never remembered, but suddenly he heard the judge say that the case against him was dismissed and that he was free.

He left the court with Father Binamet guiding him and walked out into the first snowstorm of the year as it blistered against Fort Smith heights from the grand sweep of the Mackenzie River. Outside was Sam. The old priest left the two and went back to the bishop's office. It was growing dark, and it took Dan days to fully realize what had happened. But the snow quickened Dan's pulse, and brightened his eyes. His plans for the gold might yet come about on time. He took Sam's hand and squeezed it. Then they embraced without embarrassment, as one, not two.

TWENTY

A soft covering of snow lay everywhere, and the skies were grey, the days shortening fast and the wind came like a whiplash from across the river. It twirled the powdered snow in thousands of miniature vortexes along the street at Fort Norman. Boots crunched and squeaked in it. People hunched up in their parkas and stood with their backs to it. It was not yet winter, but the landscape was filled with that unearthly stillness that was winter's forerunner.

Kayuk paced the floor of the fish-curing hut where he'd been enclosed since the day that Dan had left for Fort Smith. David, Dan's brother, was 11 and the dog fascinated him because he was allowed no pets. This fascination grew even though part of it rested in the fact that he wanted to show off the dog to his friends, which Dan had forbidden. Kayuk was to be their secret. And for three days he fed Kayuk while Dan remained in Fort Smith clearing up legal matters. The feeling for the dog became mutually close.

Each morning before school, David, who slept behind a

rough partition in the loft above the cabin, dressed and took out food and water. Kayuk never growled or barked. For the first two days he did not touch the food and with his pacing he spilt the water which froze on the earth floor. But on the third day the food from the previous two days had gone when David slid back the fish-house door. Dan had tied Kayuk with a rope to one of the drying racks in case he bolted through the door when David opened it, but David closed it behind him and put down the pickerel so that he could make sure the rope was still attached.

The dog still paced noiselessly on its huge paws. David put out his hand in the grey light and felt the animal slip under it. He picked up the pickerel and threw it in the dog's path, but Kayuk seemed to make an effort to avoid going near it. The path he was wearing with his walking circled out away from the food.

David sat and cupped his chin in his hands. He put his elbows on his left knee. His right, which always being limp since he was attacked by polio, was buckled under him. His eyes were screwed up in concentration. He could see the dog clearly now, and the size of it still amazed him. It was the biggest dog he'd ever seen. Surely, it was also the strongest. He counted the steps it took as it paced. Seventeen steps with the front paws in each direction. He looked into its face and tried to stare it out, as he had learned to do with rabbits. You could scare them into a coma.

But this was a dog with a will. One day, perhaps, Dan would let him harness Kayuk into a sleigh and see how he pulled. No one used dog sleighs any more, as the snowmobile had taken over. Dogs were used only for sport, racing and recreation, much like people in the south used horses. But somehow this made them more attractive to David, especially Kayuk.

The dog's eyes caught his at each turn for a flash of a second and then David lost them. It was a matter of time, who would give up, the boy or the dog? But it was the dog who won. Perhaps, thought David, it had known it was going to win when he started the contest. But if it had been Dan, Dan would have won. Dan was as strong as the dog, much stronger. There was no one he knew stronger than Dan. And he, David, was only Dan's small brother. And because of his leg he could never be as strong as Dan. But that didn't matter. He would have other strengths. A dog like this could be one of them.

His eyes, now on the roof of the hut, and his hands sagging across his knees, he imagined himself sitting on a sleigh at the New Year's Day races, with Kayuk pulling him across the line to victory. He imagined Kayuk pulling him into the woods and with the shotgun from the corner of the cabin, hunting a bear. There was no limit to what a boy could do with a dog like Kayuk.

He knelt and crawled nearer, running his hand over the animal's nose, along its back and giving the sweeping tail a playful jerk at the end.

"Tonight," David whispered, "tonight, Kayuk, I'll come back. Maybe bring you something sweet, heh?"

The dog continued on its path. David rose slowly. At the door, he turned hoping to see the animal start to eat the fish, but it didn't.

"I'll be back with a big surprise, tonight," he repeated.

He broke into a half-run which was all he could do and made it into the cabin just as his mother was rising from the bed in the corner by the fire. He took off his parka and slipped out of his mukluks. The fire needed wood. He poked a flame into it and placed a new log onto the embers. His mother came forward, rubbing her hands together in the icy air. She had dark skin with brown spots on it on the backs of her hands but her palms were almost white. This last month, with the troubles of Dan, had taken the strength out of her. She moved slowly without purpose.

"There's some bannock in the bin, David."

"I'll take some bread, Mom," he answered, reaching into the bread bin which stood permanently on the oilcloth of the kitchen table.

"Won't you take an egg? There's some in the straw."

David shook his head and started to bite on the hardened end of bread. His mother bent over the fire, pushing the kettle onto the hob. He saw her lift the front of her nightdress to the knees to let in the warmer air. Then she rubbed her eyes until David could hardly see them. Her face was like seal leather, grey and filled with tiny cracks across it. Her hair was like pepper. David wondered if she had always looked like this, or whether at one time she'd been young. He couldn't imagine it. Perhaps when his father had been around she was young. But he could hardly remember that either. He was the second youngest of the ten children. His sister Marie was away in Catholic boarding-school in Inuvik. He would be there too if it wasn't for his leg. Instead he stayed home. Dan told him it was better because he could look after their mother. He tried to do this, but she would not be looked after. She rarely ate. She drank endless cups of tea and smoked all day. Most days one of his elder sisters came. But they didn't clean up or anything. They usually brought grandchildren, babies with diapers and shitty arses for his mother to look after.

Yet his mother must have been glad to have him around. She would send him on errands and if he was late from school she would tell him off in her sing-song voice.

In some ways he was glad that he wasn't being sent away to board-school like the others. The small, old school here was run by Father Binamet and it had in it other children with some sort of reason for staying home, either sickness or parent trouble. Take Jamie, for instance. Jamie lived with his brother who helped out at the Bay store. Jamie had no parents. Never remembered having any. And he was tough and David's best friend. He died to tell Jamie about Kayuk.

At last he finished the bread, moistening the last piece by licking it and swallowing quickly.

His mother said, "You'd best come back at lunch. I'm going to make a mess of stew." She coughed through her hand and moved slowly towards him, her legs still grey with the cold. She took an old jacket off the back of a wooden chair and put it round her shoulders, pulling the chair nearer the fire. David wondered whether she'd remember about lunch. Some days he'd come home and she would still be sitting there, with maybe Gerald and Willie crawling at her feet. The only one who could handle her was Dan. Dan could handle anyone. And with all this fuss they were making, he had to. Dan never spoke to David about it, but David heard lots. And he hardly believed a word of it.

Now that the news on Dan's acquittal was around, David guessed that the strangers would be coming back to town. There was Ziegel, for instance, and the Slavey who was his friend. They had gone up river, out to Yellowknife, when Dan had left for Fort Smith. But David bet they'd be back this week. Unless it was getting too cold for them.

He took down the parka and worked his gimpy leg into his boot.

"See if you can get a pickerel or two out of Manger on your way. I thought we had some, but they've gone."

"I will, Mom."

At school he met Jamie. And coming home at lunch he clean forgot about the pickerel. At the door of the cabin Jamie said, "You got a cat in there, David?"

"Nope."

"Then you've been around a dog because you've got hairs on your parka."

David looked down guiltily. "I haven't so!"

"I can't see them now. But in class the light caught them."

"Well, is that so? Must have got them somewhere." David wanted so much to tell. It was bursting inside. He saw the look on Jamie's face. It was screwed up in disbelief.

Quickly he went inside and slammed the door. He heard Jamie crunch away in the snow. His mother had made stew and he was hungry. In the middle of it he slipped several pieces of meat under the table into the garbage for Kayuk.

His mother saw and slapped him hard across the side of his

face where it hurt.

"Don't you go throwing away good food. We are not made of food in here, you little bugger," she said.

"It was gristle."

"Like hell it was. There's no gristle in this. It's reindeer. You do it again, Davyboy, and I'll lam you one, real hard."

Even so he managed to put the scrapings from the two plates into the garbage after eating.

He warmed himself by the fire, and the thought about telling Jamie came to the surface again. It was unbearable, an ache. But it was dangerous. Dan had told him. Yet, David knew the dog wasn't to be feared. Hadn't he touched it? Stroked its back, and let it run under his hand?

Then it happened. In a sudden outburst he could contain the secret no longer. Outside the school he said, "Jamie, you are right about the hair. I've got something to show you."

"Show me now."

"No. Tonight—after supper. As soon as it gets real dark."

"Why can't I see now?"

"Because you will tonight. And you're not to tell. Not to tell even your brother. Promise?"

"I promise. But what is it?"

Jamie pushed him against the door. "I can't tell. Wait till tonight."

"All right. But it had better be something good . . ."

The two boys went into the school. Jamie bothered him all that afternoon wanting to know what he was going to see. Now David wished he had not told him. He began to wonder how he could get out of it. He wasn't frightened of Jamie, even though he was bigger. But he didn't like looking foolish. The dog was his secret—for Dan and he must try to keep it in spite of his sudden outburst.

After school, David called into the Bay for the pickerel. Jamie waited outside. When he came out Jamie said, "What time shall I come?"

"I don't think you'd better come," said David.

"Why not?"

"I changed my mind."

"You made a promise. I promised not to tell and you promised to show me."

"I can't. My brother made me swear a secret." David could see from Jamie's eyes that the more he tried to keep the secret, the more the other boy wanted to know.

The two boys stood in the street, their feet sticking to the snow under them and waited.

"If you don't show me, David, I'll tell everyone and I'll beat you up," Jamie said suddenly.

"Then beat me. Come on. Do it now. I'm not scared. So go on!"

The other boy tried another tack.

"Your brother wouldn't mind if you told me."

"He would so. I swore." David went on, "Are you going to beat me up, then?"

"No. I can't. You're a cripple."

"That don't make no difference, Jamie."

Jamie looked at his feet. He shifted from one to another in shame at what he'd said. "I didn't mean that. Sorry."

"I want you to stay my friend."

"Me too." Jamie grinned. "So I'll come tonight?"

David broke into a smile. "OK. Come tonight. At six. After supper."

David waited for Jamie to disappear and then picked up a stone and threw it into the Mackenzie, watching it skitter across the ice as if it were bouncing away from the cold surface. He thought of Dan. He had let him down. He felt his stomach turn. Dan was the best brother in the world, and he'd made a promise. He wished he could undo what he had done, but the frustrating part was that he couldn't. The only way was to go out to feed Kayuk early and to go up to bed afterwards so that his mother answered the door when Jamie appeared.

He placed the fish in its newspaper wrapping on the oilcloth and went over to stoke up the stove again. His mother was sitting on the same chair near the table. Her face was asleep. Worn out. Her prominent hands were laid flat on the table and the cup in the nape of her throat looked larger than ever when she sat forward.

He said, "Are you going to cook the pickerel? I had them put it on the tab. Manger said it was all right. He says to bring back the box you had the reindeer in and he'll give you some more."

"Good. Did he say what it would be?"

"No. But Dan has some arrangement with him. I heard him tell him to take care of you. Are you sure you don't want me to put the fish in the pan?"

"What's your hurry, Davyboy?"

"Jamie's coming. I got things to do first." He stooped to pick up the garbage can. "I'll take this out now." He moved to the door. It was still light. In a month it would be pitch-black at this time. He put the garbage on the roof. And he added the two spare pickerel. On the roof was a box with odd bits of food in it. Most people used the roof as a refrigerator in the winter. It was safe from the wolves and from September to the end of May was a deep freeze. He wanted to wait until dark to go back into the woods to the fish hut and feed Kayuk, but he must hurry along supper so that he could finish and not make his mother suspicious.

He was glad that Dan had entrusted the secret to him, and not even told his mother. He understood why. His mother had a bad memory and might blurt something out to one of his sisters.

When he came inside the cabin again, his mother was frying the fish. He ate it with some bannock, while she watched him over the top of her tea mug.

"You're getting big, Davyboy," she said.

"Ain't you going to eat?"

"Later," she answered as she always did. "I mean you'll soon be as tall as Dan."

Her talk reminded him and brought back the stomach pain, and he hurriedly pushed his plate into the steel sink and let it slide under the grey water. After he'd fed Kayuk, he'd collect some ice off the river and bring it in to thaw in the big bucket on the stove, and then they'd have clean water.

"I'm going to the toilet, Mom," he said as he opened the door. "Leave the rest. I'll clean up when I've got some ice."

He slammed the door. He was sure it was not yet six o'clock. But it was dark enough. He made tracks through the piece of land they called the yard and up past the toilet towards the fish-hut.

It stood among some trees, birches, which had been used in his father's time to smoke the fish for winter. He had the garbage bag in one hand and some snow on a tin plate in the other. He undid the lock and slid back the door.

Kayuk was still pacing. The fish was gone. He put down the plate of snow and undid the garbage, letting the reindeer meat roll into the dust near Kayuk's continuous path. He saw the dog's nostril flare slightly.

"Good boy," he said. "Good boy. Got you a good supper." The dog stopped and came over and licked his hand. He smiled in joy.

"You want Dan, don't you. He'll be back soon."

The dog sniffed away from him and started to lick the meat all over, its mouth dripping saliva at the sides. David patted its head and hugged it to him. The dog wagged its tail, brushing its own nest.

He leaned over and carefully undid the rope, rubbing Kayuk's neck where the continual pulling on it had worn away the fur in the three days it had been with him. The rope swung back and the dog shook itself as if throwing off invisible water. He patted it again and knelt, his bad leg under him, so that he could watch the huge animal eat.

Kayuk was half-way through when David felt Jamie's hand on his shoulder. He was completely startled and Kayuk let out a warning growl.

Jamie stood back against the door.

"Thought you'd fool me by coming early. I've been watching

your place since you went in," he said.

"I had to keep my promise to Dan."

"Oh, sure. What's so great about a dog anyway?" said Jamie in a voice that sounded miffed.

"He's a great dog. Can't you see, Jamie?"

"I guess he's all right. Better not let him free. Johnny Grover's got a gun that'll kill him in no time."

"I ain't letting him free," said David. "No sir, not until Dan arrives tomorrow or the day after."

Jamie sat beside him. David felt foolish. He'd sure built it all up into a big thing. Now he was going to try to play it down a bit.

"He's very friendly. Go on, Jamie. Give him a pat."

Kayuk was just finishing his meal. Jamie looked scared. "You sure?" He swallowed. "Then what's the rope for?"

"In case he escapes, and besides I just undid it." David said, "Go on. Pat him."

Jamie put one hand on David's shoulder and David felt the weight. He said, "Ouch."

The dog sprang while Jamie was half up towards it. Even at that time it was obvious to David that it thought Jamie was hurting him. It landed on Jamie's back and its teeth ripped into the boy's jacket. Jamie rolled on his back. He was yelling and screaming enough to bring the whole settlement. David was beating into the fur around Kayuk's neck, but he couldn't pull him off. Jamie yelled, "Help me, Dave. Get a gun. Shoot him. He's a wolf. A wolf."

David began to speak calmly to Kayuk, "Hey boy, get off. It's all right. It's all right. Come on, boy."

He felt the muscles in the dog's shoulders start to relax and the jaw soften. He pulled Kayuk free. David then flung himself onto Jamie to protect him. Then he pulled himself off and took a look at the arm. The dog had grazed the flesh. The clothing was badly ripped but he could see the teeth marks were small.

"He had a fright. He thought you were attacking me."

Jamie was shouting again and there was a noise from the settlement. People were coming. Jamie sat holding his shoulder and crying. David tried to shake some sense into him.

Then Jim Gardner's face came round the door. David stood up and peered into the back of the hut, hoping he could tie up Kayuk. But Kayuk had gone. Two others came in behind him. Then a couple of gossipy women.

David heard himself say, "It's all right. He isn't hurt much. Take him to the nurse."

"It was a wolf!" said Jamie. "It was a wolf. The animal is wolf."

"No. He isn't," said David. "He is a dog."

Two men lifted up Jamie and carried him to the nurse. Soon they had all gone. After a time David dried his eyes and made his way to the cabin. As he climbed the steep, ladder stairs to his bed, his mother was still sitting on the chair by the table. She had hardly moved since he left.

He lay awake most of that night, wondering how he could have come to let out his brother's secret.

TWENTY-ONE

By the time that Dan was due to arrive from Fort Smith, most of the settlement knew about the wolf-dog which had attacked Jamie Post in the fish-hut, although most could not understand to whom the animal belonged. David kept his mouth shut, explaining that he had found the dog. Jamie got a rabies injection and a pat on the head from the nurse for the wound was very slight. He too kept his promise.

Jim Gardner and Johnny Grover suspected that the dog belonged to Dan, although that didn't worry them. The main thing was to get rid of it before it did anyone any real harm. Wolves and wild dogs always returned to the place from which they were getting food. The garbage dump a mile downstream was a favourite place. Another was the bush around the abandoned mine. Among the stunted pines there were rabbits, wild mink and muskrat. The place also provided easy access to the settlement itself.

When Dan got out of the plane he was not aware of what had happened. Kayuk was not in his thoughts. Sam was. Fort

Smith was one hundred and fifty miles up river towards Yellowknife and when he took the plane north to Fort Norman, Sam had taken another plane, south to Yellowknife. They'd had two full days together and with the unofficial blessing of the old priest, Father Binamet, they had rejoiced between themselves. Sam had promised to come north again before Christmas, which seemed already on the horizon to Dan what with the snow and the bite in the wind. Sam had also tried again to dissuade him from going out to stake. And again he had tactfully stuck to his point.

"They seen the dog again," said Manger as Dan and the priest stood outside the Bay, "but you didn't hear of it up there, I guess."

Moments later Dan stood beside David whom he'd met coming out of school for lunch.

"You are going to beat me."

"Just tell me what happened?"

"He thought Jamie was attacking me and he went for him."

"And then?"

"He ran off."

"Where?"

"I dunno. I've looked, Dan, Everywhere."

"You must have some idea."

"I looked at night because they've been watching me."

"Who's been watching?"

"Jim Gardner and Grover. Grover's been splitting up logs out by the fish-hut. He's always got his rifle."

Dan looked at his brother's eyes. They were heavy from lack of sleep. His usually rounded features were drawn and his hands were showing the signs of his nervous apprehension.

"You've been worrying about it then?"

"Mostly about what you'd say, Dan."

The two of them sat down on the end of the woodpile Dan had cut for his mother earlier that year. It was snowing again and the skies were leadened with further heaviness. It was more private here, yet Dan could see Gardner now a couple of hundred yards away, sitting on his snowmobile, the engine turned off and lighting a cigarette. His rifle was on his back.

"Blow your nose," he said to David, "Manger said they've seen Kayuk again."

David blew into Dan's handkerchief. "Maybe. But it didn't sound like Kayuk. They put out some meat at the dump. And some animal took it. Could have been a bear."

"Could have been Kayuk."

"There's more. Something killed Oslen's cat. The Persian cat. The old tom-cat. Kayuk wouldn't do that."

Dan thought a moment. He, too, didn't believe he would, but you could never be sure. A wolf was a wolf and Kayuk was at least half wolf. A wolf which had saved his life. The thought triggered the recent memories of the fact that he had also killed a man up there in the bush. He wondered how long it would be before the memory would not hurt. It would certainly be a long time before he erased the feeling of the warmth of the dead man's hands. No. Even if Kayuk had killed here at Fort Norman, that was no reason to let him die, too.

"All right, David. We've gotta find him. That's all."

"I'll do anything. I mean it. Anything, Dan."

"You go and get some food."

"Beat me. Hit me."

"No."

"I'd feel much better if you did."

"Go eat lunch. Tell Mom I'll be bringing something for supper. And go to bed. Tonight we may go on a hunt."

That night they took off for the old ruined hut where Dan had originally put the dog, up the river by the hot spring. The snow was new and there were no signs. Dan brushed away the top layers near the open hut door, but there was no mark of the dog's paws. Inside there was some dogshit, but it had been there since Kayuk had lived there. The place didn't smell of dog. Dan went outside and called into the bush. They waited half an hour or so in case the dog had heard and was some way off. Then they went on up to the hot spring, calling and tracking all the way.

It was bitterly cold, but it had stopped snowing. There was now a moon and some very high cumulus clouds. In spite of the cold Dan could not resist the opportunity. He stripped off and plunged into the warm waters. He urged David to do the same, but there was shyness about the boy which he understood. The water ran over Dan's body, and the muscles began to relax. He felt suspended in warmth and softness, as if he had Sam's arms enveloping him all over. He kicked lazily, letting his thoughts drift, while David sat in his parka with the hood half hiding his face, watching.

Life was getting good again. He had been living, even feeding his family, from Ziegel's pocket. It was not free food because Ziegel would end up with the lion's share of this one claim. But Dan had the other claim, which only Sam knew about, and that was what he was basing his future on. He had argued about it all with Sam, and to show her that he meant to carry out his plans even though she objected, he had drawn a simple map of both his finds, marking out where they were in relation to the settlement and to each other.

She had tucked the map in the bottom of her bag. "In case you go through with this crazy thing alone, I'll know where you are," she said.

Dan was suddenly aware of David in the water with him. The boy was swimming and laughing, the water making his long hair stick to his back in a plaster. Dan was glad. It meant the boy was shaking off his shyness. It was a step to growing up.

"Come over here and feel the heat from where it comes up," said Dan. "The water's much hotter in the middle."

David paddled over and he caught hold of the boy's wrist, the warm young body passing him swiftly. He was lithe and strong. David was going to be a big guy in spite of his leg. Taller than Dan. Dan straightened out the thin leg, where the polio had withered the muscles.

"If you came up here every day, you'd soon be able to use that leg again properly," Dan said.

"I'll do it, Dan, if you want me to."

They swam around for twenty minutes and then Dan pulled his brother to the rocks and they dressed hurriedly. The moon had disappeared and some more snow was falling. The skies had blackened and the wind whipped up. They wrapped their parkas tightly around them and zipped up the hods. Dan called for Kayuk, but his voice came back at him empty.

It was about two o'clock in the morning when they reached the settlement again and the snow was blowing almost level from the north-west. They had to lean into it to walk. It was catching the edges of the cabins and piling up in drifts towards the windows. Pretty soon it would cover the cabins and they'd have to dig a path to the door. All you'd be able to see would be humps of snow with chimneys coming from them.

Their mother was asleep when they came in. She lay, a small crumpled heap under the quilt Grandma had made, in the bed in the corner. Her right hand was under her head and her other hand lay like a large brown stain on the quilt.

Dan motioned David up the ladder to bed. His bed, too, was in the loft. But he was not ready. He drew up a chair, put his feet on the top of the stove and let the warm air float up his pants along his legs. He lit a cigarette. He wondered what he could do to help his mother get out of this filthy hovel. He would have to be tactful, for she had lived here since she was first married. Lived here through ten children. It was her home, but it was killing her slowly. It was overpowering. She had no energy even to clean it. Perhaps it would be better to move in some electricity, appliances and some new furniture. She had always wanted a new sofa. For as long as he could remember it had been on her mind. Each New Year she would say that this was to be the year when she would have a new sofa.

Dan must have dozed off in front of the heat. For he heard his mother call. She was rarely fully asleep.

She said, "Johnny Grover was here. They seen that wolf again. It come near the priest's chicken-house. Killed one, Johnny said."

"That wasn't my dog, Ma."

"I wish you'd told me you had it, I'd have got it shot and done with." She coughed into her hand. "Now they're going to have a hunt. Tomorrow night, Johnny says."

Dan stood up and threw the burned out cigarette into the stove. "Who's going to have a hunt?"

"Johnny and Jim Gardner."

Dan thought a second. Then he said, "I'll be along with them then."

He went up the ladder to join his brother who was already asleep.

TWENTY-TWO

Kayuk smelt the beginnings of winter in the wind. He had been travelling deeper into the bush, weaving his way through the undergrowth available so that his trail would be impossible to find. He doubled back on his tracks every once in a while. He sprang across frozen streams, to break the scent, and he buried his droppings, pushing soil over them with his nose.

Kayuk had hated the hut. But he had been shut in worse places. More than the hut, he hated the fact that Dan had disappeared. He never felt love for anyone, even Dan. It was something he didn't understand. But Dan was part of him and to have him go away like that was to lose part of himself.

Kayuk's first objective was to make sure no one found him. His second task was to find Dan. For three days he had made sure no one would find him. Now he was about to turn round and start finding Dan. He had not eaten, because the leftovers of the animal would give a trace. He had licked the snow and used the new-found leanness in his muscles to make him better at what he was doing. But he was also now very hungry.

He stood now, facing the wind, his nostrils twitching. But there was no scent in the wind. He pawed the soil under him in frustration. The scent of man was so strong he could decipher it, decode it, isolate it, from a thousand other smells. But in the wind there was no trace of man.

He had printed indelibly on his memory the scent of Dan, one particular man out of the thousands of others. He had done this when he had been digging up Dan's rocks for him in the big place to the south. If there had been a trace of that he would have detected it immediately and it would have given him a direction. But there was no scent.

He stood on a small rise in the land, no more than three times the height of his shoulders, but it was enough to let him sniff above the bush, for the trees were small. The snow fell on his head and along his back. It made the hackles rise on his neck and the dark, thick undercoat of his fur which lay beneath the outer layer of grey fur, tighten and form a mat against the cold.

He was sure that the way back to the settlement and to food was in the direction of the wind. He had run north with the wind on the left side of him for the first day, so that his smell blew away into the breeze and scattered. Then he had turned completely away from the wind, running with it. This meant that unless men had been able to follow him north, even with the help of animals, they would not have been able to take up his trail. But now he had to reverse the order and to start back to the settlement by travelling east.

He was in good shape despite the hunger. The cold helped. It gave him an immense sense of energy reserve. But he lacked the drive. It was something he would recover in time. He lay down and let the snow fly against him. He put his head on his paws and licked his lips, moistening his mouth. He tried to understand what drew him to Dan. It was an immense need.

After a while, he rose and shook off the snow. He was so sure about the direction that he plunged down the steep rise into the small valley of snow. His legs went in to the shoulders and he swam forward in a shower of powder. As he forced his way out on the other side, he could not at first find the wind. It seemed to be coming from many places. He thought it was to his left and he ran that way. But the right side of his face was colder and when he turned his nose it seemed to come from the right.

Running, jumping the banks, trying to make time because of the hunger that was eating into him he suddenly felt the wind full on his left side. Maybe he had turned too far. He veered left again and there seemed to be no wind.

He stopped and raked his head, turning it slowly from the warmer air to the colder and back again. He was standing in a small clearing. He put his nose to the snow and dug a hole, breathing into it to melt the ice, and trying to reach the earth. When he reached it, he licked it. There was a moss spoor in the earth. It tasted sweet to him. But he knew that to lick it would give him stomach-ache. The earth was filled with parasites which would sicken him. He circled the grove with his nose close to the snow and eventually came back to the hole he had dug. He made another circle, and yet another. Always he came back to the hole.

At each turn he sniffed again. The wind was so faint and the snow falling so straight, that he still didn't know. He took one more turn of the circle. From the north end, he thought for a split second, that there was something, but it turned out to be the smell of pine sap. It was a great hindrance to a dog, as it blotted out all other smells.

He went back to the hole and cleaned out the snow which had fallen since. Then he lay on it. It was a marker.

He was lost. It had never happened to him before, even though he knew of such things. He lay flat over the hole, trying to make himself into as low a profile as he could. Soon the snow would cover everything except his nose tip. He would be safe until the wind started again.

Kayuk went to sleep in his white blanket and he thought in that sleep that he had found Dan again and that they were both swimming in the water at the pool. It was warm and friendly, in spite of the rotten-egg smell. Dan urged him to get a stick and to jump into the pool for it. In his sleep, his need for Dan grew even greater than the hunger in his stomach, which was painful now. At times he woke and remained in half sleep, thinking he was fully awake.

Kayuk woke and it was night. There was no snow falling but the air was filled with it above. Even though he had slept, he was tired. He started to walk to the west again and he walked most of the night. There were very few trees in these parts, no shelter and no scents. Occasionally there was a small hill of snow and underneath were rocks. They were not the rocks he knew. They seemed to be brittle and had no salt in them. Once he thought he smelt a weasel or a mink, but it turned out to be an old scent, from last year. Then again, later, he came upon a lynx's lair in the side of a rocky slope. He padded up to it to see if there was food or if the lynx could be trapped, but the place was empty and the few bones dried out and useless.

He padded on towards the west and when the sun came up he looked up at it and howled. It was a lone call for help. But something in him said he should give it. He was very tired and the hunger now was past pain. It had gone into weakness. His back legs wavered as he walked and he had to drag them along at times. His head imagined scents and sights. He could not trust it. He was very tired.

Finally, when the sun had been up enough to start to warm him and bring on a pant, he looked up. Ahead was a cliff. Ahead was a smell. It was animal, not man. He was not afraid. He started to climb slowly, dragging his legs.

Then he realised that he had walked all night and all day and was back at the lair of the lynx. The animal blinked at him from the front of the cave. He could not summon up the energy to fight. It seemed useless. If he won, there would be food perhaps but it was better to reserve his energy to try to walk. He turned tail and with a snarl went on his way. His back legs stiffened and finally he came to a stop. He fell in a heap and lay almost totally exhausted on the snow. The sun had gone and the day was now dark again. He saw around him trees, but he knew there were no trees. He saw again people. He even smelt people and tried to snuggle into an invisible form, but there were not any people. Once he imagined he saw Dan and his tail gave an involuntary wag, but Dan was not there.

Kayuk's stomach ached now that he was not using his remaining energy to walk. His back legs also were very painful. He had to keep turning over to rest.

He never knew how long he rested like that but it was totally dark when he woke and he rose and trudged on to the west. The wind was up again now and he thought he could smell many things, but his nose was fooling him.

The pads of his paws began to bleed just as dawn came. He left tracks that even the stupid coward of a lynx could follow. He licked the snow balls out from between his toes and it eased the pain. The blood tasted hot and good. That day as the sun went down he came upon a frozen river, which at first he thought was the great river. He bounded up using energy and even barking. But it turned out to be a small piece of water. It led south-west, so he followed it. There were occasional minks in the banks and he tried to catch them in a half-hearted manner, walking down the middle of the ice and taking a run as they scurried to their nests at the edge of the banks. In the end it was too strenuous for him and he gave up and went back to the frozen river banks where the snow was less hard on his pads.

He walked until he was dragging his back legs again. It had become bitter cold, even with his fur it was hard to shelter. Ice formed on his back and along the edge of his stomach. He had to keep turning and pulling it off with his teeth. He could see a hill up ahead. Normally it would have taken him a few minutes to reach. He stopped readying himself to summon the energy to climb to its peak and his bowels began to empty onto the snow. There was blood in it and he nosed the acrid-smelling stuff under the snow.

He started to pull up the hill by using only his front paws to lever himself and letting his back paws take the weight between the steps. But the ground was loose under the snow and it fell back on him, tumbling him down again, so that he had to try several times before he had managed to make even a few feet. He was by now one-third of the way up. He stood, dizzily holding onto the shifting earth under the snow and looked down. If he fell he would die. He waited. He thought that there was a hope that over the hill he would smell man. He told himself that it would be the scent of Dan.

He began to edge his way further up. Step by step he came nearer. The pain in his back legs had gone, but they were useless. His mouth was spitting blood and his stomach had started to swell. He knew this was a fatal sign. If he didn't have food soon, he would die.

By sunrise he was a few feet from the top. He took it a step at a time. As his front paws came over the rise, he realised he had no more strength left to pull up his back feet. Yet if he let his grip go, he would surely fall.

Then he smelt something that gave him the strength he needed. He smelt his fellow creatures. Dogs, he thought in his befuddled state. He yanked himself over the edge and onto the small plate-shaped top of the hill which was so cold it was blown almost free of snow. There was no living creature on the hill. He lay down, painting and exhausted. Then he smelt it again. It wasn't dogs. It was wolves. Wolves were up ahead. Not on the hill perhaps, but just over it. They were sure to smell his blood. He had no more strength. He would put up a fight, but it would be a poor one, even though wolves were usually cowards. He was doomed.

Kayuk went to sleep. When he woke the moon had taken the place of the sun and he was surrounded by empty sky. Then he remembered he was on top of a hill.

He lay and stretched his body. His legs were stiff, but they seemed better. He pulled himself to his feet and crouched looking over the other side of the hill.

A mother wolf huddled into a small hole half-way down the

hill with a cub. He came across to the other side of the hill which was where he came up and he saw the male wolf threading its way towards him over the blood-stained snow.

He turned back and started down past the mother wolf. Normally he would have chased her from the den. But now he ignored her and listened to her howl. He paused nearby to straighten his hind legs and in that second the male wolf reached the hilltop and leaped. It landed on Kayuk's back. It was a foolish thing to do for Kayuk had only to collapse and fall into the snow beside him. He turned snarling. The wolf circled him. The circles got smaller. He waited for the leap to come again.

The wolf was big, but normally no match for him. It had smelt blood and knew that Kayuk was therefore weak. Kayuk tucked his head into his neck and stiffened his fur so that when the animal bit it would take mostly fur. He lifted his head now, showing his neck. He knew the wolf would go for the jugular.

It did. And it hit the fur. Kayuk put up a paw and pushed. He managed to get the wolf on its back. His weight was enough to hold it down. He bit hard. First on the right ear and then on the throat. He felt his teeth go in and he tasted blood. He had no strength to finish off the animal. He gave it a rip and tore the flesh down the side of its neck. It yelped and ran. He staggered to the bottom of the hill, safe in the knowledge that it was too scared to follow. He licked the ice and blood off his paws.

Then he smelt something which filled him with joy. Ahead lay a seeming wasteland of ice and the dim outline of trees and cabins. The scent twitched in his nostrils and made him quiver. It brought strength. It was that unmistakable smell, of man, animals and the mixture of good and bad that he had grown up with. It was home. Not his home, but Dan's home.

The particularly strong scent was of chickens. He padded down the hill waiting for the night-time to attack across the ice for his well-earned meal.

TWENTY-THREE

The steam rose from the men's clothing as they stood in their red flannel shirts around the stove at the back of the Bay store. There were Johnny Grover, Jim Gardner, Manger and Chief Andrews. They gathered, holding their hands above the old pot-belly stove as if they were sacrificial priests around some altar.

The old chief, tall, gaunt, all sinew. His face sculpted over the bones, his hair like the snow itself, hanging in a shoulder cape.

"If the priest lost a chicken, there's likely more'n one of 'em," he said.

Johnny Grover nodded. "There was dog in him, but he might be travelling with a pack. If we get the great sonofabitch, the rest will scatter." Johnny Grover was the smallest of the four, and the toughest. His personality was shrivelled into him behind a walnut-like face. He and the fat man, Jim Gardner were official hunters. Chief Andrews had employed them to keep the place clean of predators.

"I made the trap this afternoon," said Johny. "Jim and me have it set up."

"We're going to set up another on the hill behind. A live trap."

"But it ain't baited yet," added Jim. "We need some beef. Ripe if you got it, Bill," he said to Manger.

"That he's got," said the chief, and the men laughed. Bill Manger rose without humour to get the meat from the store. As he opened the door, Dan appeared.

"I'm coming with you," Dan said.

"There's six of us already, Cunard, Rod and Arnie Nickelsen is comin'," said Jim.

Dan took off his parka and placed it on the hooks with the others to dry out. Standing in his shirt and braces by the stove, the others made room for him to warm.

"I'm coming because it's my dog," said Dan.

"Your dog? Better you shouldn't be there," said the chief.

"He's not a killer. He saved my life. I'm going to take him away, up to the hills."

"He'll be back, Dan. One day he'll turn on you, or your friend."

"I don't want him killed."

"It's an order, Dan. Not only because of the boy. I think that was an accident. But because of the chicken and the cat."

"Then let me do it," said Dan.

There was a pause and Manger came back with some hamburger steak.

Johnny said, "You stay away. We know how to handle it."

"Then why are Cunard and Rod coming?"

"They volunteered," said Manger quickly. "They want some shooting practice."

Dan looked at the chief. The old man looked like a saint, but he was too old for the job. Dan could see Manger was buying him off too.

"All right," said the chief. "Take my place, Dan." He turned and the men started to pull on their parkas. Johnny was examining the barrel of his hunting rifle.

"We're meeting up behind the priest's chicken hut in twenty minutes."

It was not yet fully dark when Dan ran across the street and through the ditch to his mother's cabin. The skies were cloudy and heavy but at times clear. He slammed the door of the cabin angrily, wondering what Cunard and Rod had paid to get in on the hunt.

"Mum, where's David?" he asked, taking up the rifle from the corner by the stove.

"He went out."

Dan was filling his pockets with cartridges. "When did he go?"

"After school," she said, sipping her tea. "Are they going to hunt that wolf-dog?"

"Yes."

"What are you going to do? Stop 'em killing it? You are crazy. You'll end up in jail again. You're crazier than I thought."

"I guess I am," he said. "If you see David, don't tell him where I am."

"I won't. It's plumb crazy. When the chief gives an order to kill a dog, it has to be done. It's the law. Jail," she repeated, savouring the word around her toothless gums, "jail. You'll get it yet. Wild idiot boy."

"Shut up, Mum."

He put the rifle on his shoulder and pulled the parka hood over his head. He looked over at his mother. She was huddled by the table, the dishes left from lunch around her and a magazine on her lap. Nature was not playing fair with her. It was letting her live on long after she needed life. She no longer had any purpose. The rainbow had disappeared over the hill.

He went and put his arm around her. She was still his mother, and Nature didn't fool around with people for too long. She'd soon be dead.

"If you had a chance of getting anything you wanted, Ma,

what would you get?"

"That's a crazy question. Foolish."

"Anything you want?"

"Anything?" Her lips crinkled into a smile. "I never thought. I never thought about it, Dannyboy."

"Yes, you have, Ma," he said.

"Yeh, I suppose so. The sofa. A new sofa."

"At New Year's I'll get you one."

She smiled again. "Oh sure. And a hat like the Queen wears with fancy shoes."

"I will, Ma. You just think about it. Imagine it over there. I will get it."

He rarely kissed her these days. He leaned over and kissed her on the forehead. Then he left the cabin and made his way to the front of the Bay store.

The others were there. Rod came over and shook hands, Cunard shadowing him as usual.

"I hear the dog's yours."

"It's the one Sam found in Yellowknife." Dan said no more.

Johnny Grover divided them into three pairs, and announced that Manger wasn't coming now. Dan was paired with Johnny. Rod and Cunard went together. Jim Gardner took Arnie Nickelsen, a lanky Swede who had a cabin half a mile up towards Norman Wells.

They moved through the bush just as it was getting dark, the stubbly growth of the trees at times no higher than themselves. At last they were on the side of the range of hills north-east of Fort Norman. Beneath them was the bed of a frozen stream which ran into the great river. They placed themselves on either side of a gully which formed a basin half-way up the stream.

The moon was out. It was still occasionally covered with dark cloud. Dan could see the trap from where he crouched in the snow. He could also see the settlement below, only four hundred yards away, Johnny had chosen the perfect place for a trap because an animal would make its way down the edges of the river bed towards the settlement. At the end it would meet up with the chicken-house which Father Binamet had built. The wind was blowing off the iced surface of the great river towards them, so the scent of the chicken and the other smells of the settlement were being tasted by any animals in the hills around the gully.

The trap down by Father Binamet's place was a series of stakes, each about four feet long and driven into the ground. They formed a tepee at the top. the meat lay at the back and as the animal touched it, it fired the cage door closed.

He thought hard. He'd come thinking that at the last resort he would shoot Kayuk. But he knew now he had to stop the slaughter. There had to be a way. He wondered where David had gone.

TWENTY-FOUR

David could see the hunters from where he sat. He was farther up the river and had spent the hours since getting out of school making his way through the bush as he watched Johnny and Jim setting the traps. He was using an old walking-stick to hobble along. He was now pretty cold, but he told himself that it would soon be over.

He must have been over a hundred yards away from the hunters. The nearest was probably Dan who had his back to him as he and Johnny looked down at the trap in the gully. On the other side were Cunard and Rod. He could tell, because both the inexperienced men were smoking and talking. This was something that David knew a professional hunter never did.

He must have sat watching them for half an hour, the moon going in and out of the heavy clouds, bringing contrasting dark and brightness to the evening.

He was numb, but he could not move much now. Then to his left, over his shoulder, came a noise. It was very small. A mouse might have made it. The moon came out and he saw Kayuk. He was a good way away, where the hill dipped again away from the hunters who were protected from the sound.

He started to run towards the animal, travelling through the uneven snow. Kayuk was moving slowly. He seemed to be very weak, and his hind legs were dragging themselves almost drunkenly. His tail was brushing the snow and his ears were down on his head. David had a great urge to yell out in joy. He stumbled and fell. Before he could raise himself again, Kayuk was licking his neck and growling his greetings.

"Shut up. Quiet. You idiot."

He rolled in the snow and pinned Kayuk underneath him, his hand over his nose. The animal seemed to understand and so he let go the nose and hugged the dog. He was wet with blood and more blood had dried on his fur. His back legs were stiff and unbending. David took them in his hands and tried to rub back the life. They were suffering from a type of frost-bite which came when an animal's blood wasn't circulating fast enough through weakness.

"Good Kayuk! Good dog!" David kept repeating.

David stood up. "Think you can make it home?" he said. He took up his walking-stick and the two of them set off.

They had travelled only a few yards when a new and recognisable smell came to Kayuk's nostrils. Up to now he had smelt only David. Now he smelt Dan. He swerved suddenly and jumped. He was going in the direction of the gully.

David tried to grab his back and fell again. Kayuk was bounding over the snow, his hind legs working for a few steps and then letting themselves be dragged.

David moved as fast as he could. He no longer cared about being silent. He had to stop Kayuk reaching the crest of the hill and jumping towards Dan in the gully.

He stopped, ready to shout the dog's name. Then Kayuk jumped. He disappeared and a cloud of snow rose from the other side of the hill. Kayuk slid into view of the marksmen.

TWENTY-FIVE

Kayuk landed on a snow-covered rock. Even as he was in the air, he sensed something was wrong. As he landed, he saw the men. Certainly one of them was Dan, who was surely still his friend. But they all carried rifles, and the rabbit, tethered to the post, brought back a memory of danger. He stood stock-still, as still as he had when he followed Dan through the bush earlier in the year.

One of the men raised a rifle. It was the man next to Dan. The moon went behind a thick cloud. The man fired.

"I think I got him," Johnny said.

They could see little. Dan felt sick. He had heard a sound up on the hill behind him and he had temporarily turned to see. In that second, Johnny had fired.

David also heard the shot. He reached the top of the hill and jumped. Another shot rang out. It was Cunard on the other side of the gully.

"I got him too," Cunard shouted. "I've got him up on the hill there."

The shot hit David in the forearm and he rolled to a stop in the snow, not far from Dan, who was running towards him.

"Stop! Don't fire," he was yelling. But the men were not listening; they were running down into the gully to where the rabbit sat in a frightened ball, and the animal which Johnny had shot lay beside it, dead with blood making marks in the snow.

"It's a wolf," Jim shouted. "It's not the dog."

"It was Johnny's shot," said someone else.

Cunard stood beside them sheepishly.

"What the hell did you fire at, man?" Johnny said.

"Up on the hill. Something moved. It was an animal."

"You could have killed Dan or me," Johnny went on.

Dan was picking up David and bringing him down the hill. The boy was trying to make him put him down.

When he reached the group, Dan put David on the snow next to the rabbit. The wind was whipping up and the snow was piling against their legs. Dan turned to Cunard and belted him on the jaw. The man pitched forward and Dan gave him a left jab to the other side of the jaw. He fell to the snow. Then he took hold of David's hand and picked him onto his back. Johnny undid the belt on his hunting parka and tied it around David to hold him secure. Cunard lay out on the snow. Cold. Rod looked stunned. Dan started home.

Kayuk lay where he had fallen. His back legs were very painful, but he knew if he could get to the food which he smelt and into the warmth of some shelter, he would be all right.

He also knew that he should not let those other men see him. In spite of his wish to run up to Dan, he decided to dog Dan's steps all the way back to the cabin.

It was hard, slow and painful, but when Dan arrived at the door with David on his back, the dog was lying against it and his tail gave some weak flops and then he felt Dan pick him up and carry him inside beside the fire. He had never been inside a cabin before, having spent his whole life in the open. He felt unsafe and the smell was awful to him. Yet he knew he was being helped.

Dan took a look at David's arm. He took out the bottle of iodine and poured it into the bullet graze. David's hand bit into Dan's arm and the nails drew blood. Their mother was asleep in her chair, her head on the table. Dan took up a towel and ripped it up to make a bandage. Then he put David in their mother's bed and covered him over.

Dan said, "Damn fool dog. No damn fool dog is worth it."

David said, "Maybe. But Kayuk's no damn fool. He's smart."

"For a smart dog he sure gets into a lot of trouble," said Dan and he knelt to stroke the dog's head as he placed the scraps from the plates before him.

TWENTY-SIX

Through November and most of December, Fort Norman had little fresh snow. The winter set in early in October with heavy snows and the temperature hit fifty below on most nights so the original snow remained. Although the road through the settlement was bull-dozed, snow was piled on either side as high as most men's heads, and all the cabins were buried on their windward west sides. People dug tunnels to their front doors. Some, lucky enough to have a back door, never bothered to dig out the front. In this mole-like environment an active social life existed. People played poker, gambled, told stories, held musical evenings, went to the church hall to watch films and to dance to Scottish reels taught by their ancestors and Scottish traders. The children built a rink, on the flat inlet from the Mackenzie, south of the settlement, and played hockey.

Trappers, hunters and prospectors ventured out into the twenty-two-hour night to try to make a living. Most of them left in November. Some didn't return until Christmas or later, only to make another sortie in the new year. Each man's trapline was sacred. To be found raiding it was to risk death. Each man's hunting was also held in similar respect. The men who held the hunting rights and the traplines often lived on them, as much as a hundred miles from home. The traplines went in circles, returning on themselves—usually to a small shack caught in some crevasse where a man could winter alone. It was a lonely, hard life, but people who lived it rarely wanted a change. Hunting, trapping and prospecting ran in families for generations.

Dan was watched by Rod Ziegel or Cunard all the early winter weeks. One or the other found some excuse to be in Fort Norman and Dan's mother's cabin was under constant covert surveillance.

Manger had kept to his word. Food and dry goods for Dan and his family arrived regularly and Ted Ziegel was billed. From these Dan managed to stash away ample supplies without Manger's realising he was already grub-staking. Bags of dried peas, whole-wheat flour, maple syrup, canned beans and beef, eggs and sourbelly. Chocolate bars, dried fruit and vegetables, boxes of wooden matches, charcoal and a blanket. These things Dan secreted without robbing his family. They were now in the ruined cabin where Kayuk had lived on his arrival in the settlement. Dan had replaced the door and boarded up the windows, locking the place. Kayuk also spent his time there, away from the settlement, having earned a reprieve from Chief Andrews since it had become well-known that the lone wolf had done the damage to the chickens and other animals.

In early December, Dan went down river forty miles to Norman Wells, where Imperial Oil had a small oil refinery. He knew a Cree in that tiny outpost who had bought a Yamaha snowmobile and then got into a serious accident so that he couldn't use it. Dan gave the Cree one hundred and sixty dollars for its hire for the winter.

It was a big, powerful machine and it did sixty miles to the gallon. His friend also gave him two ten-gallon drums of gasoline, which he hitched behind the snowmobile on runners.

That night Dan left for Fort Norman. He took a circuitous route through the bush away from the river and he hid the vehicle in the cave near the ruined cabin.

Two days before Christmas, the sofa arrived for his mother. It came over the ice from Fort Smith on a tractor sleigh. And Manger charged that up to Ziegel. He did the same with a small radio which Dan gave to David. Ziegel was biding his time, and one day would take his pound of flesh.

Dan supposed that by that time almost everyone in the settlement knew that he was into the big time. Having a man like Ziegel behind you bought you a lot. It also made you unpopular. That didn't worry Dan. The look on his mother's face when she saw the sofa was worth it.

"What am I going to do with that?" she said, shuffling over and trying it out. "I must be going to die. God's being too good to me." After that she put the wrapping back on it to protect the bright green artificial leather she had chosen as its covering.

David took the radio to school. It was almost as good as having Kayuk to show off.

During midnight Mass on Christmas Eve, the settlement was empty. There was a carol service at the Anglican church also, and people were ushering in the feast with joy. It was not a time when anyone would want to do anything that was not with his family, thought Dan. Ziegel and Cunard had left for Yellowknife that day, probably thinking the same thoughts.

Dan dressed, put on his parka and took a small pack with dry clothing it in on his back. He left through the back door and in minutes was up-river at the cave, manœuvring the snowmobile into the grey light of the misted moon. All his provisions, including the gasoline, were on a sleigh which was hitched to the back of the snowmobile. On the front end of the sleigh he had built a wooden three-sided box and strapped it on. It was just enough to allow Kayuk to lie in. On the other side of it a bag with the tent and the charcoal stove.

Kayuk came at his call and lay in the box as if he had been

used to it as his own. There would be times when the dog could run loose beside the vehicle each day, but no animal could average the speed of the snowmobile for too long.

Dan pulled out the choke, pressed the starter and felt the engine under him burst into power. It was a sweet sound. He let in the clutch and the contraption started to move like a train across the snow to the river. It hugged the snow like a tank. Dan eased it onto the ice and turned south.

The wind hit him hard. A whip. Dan hated the wind from that moment on. It became to him a living obstacle, continually harassing him and worse than man himself. He grew to hate it and to respect it. Finally he grew to know it could win battles with him, as a superior enemy. He tucked his chin into the fur edging on the parka hood. It was colder than he expected. Perhaps he should have put on his face mask. He turned to see Kayuk's nose poking out from the side of the box. The moist, black snout looked like wet coal.

The machine was only doing about ten miles an hour. Dan didn't want to make too much noise.

He saw the settlement over his shoulder. They were coming out of Mass now. He saw the splash of light from the church door. A lot of people turned on the kerosene lamps in their cabins. Electric lights were also ablaze. It must be Christmas now, he thought. It was a good feeling. It was also a good time to be starting on a trip. He visualised his mother and David arriving home now. His mother would make tea and sit on the new sofa. He had left three letters on the table. Inside his mother's was a Christmas card and some money. Inside David's was a note telling him to look after his mother and to post the third letter. It was to Sam in Yellowknife.

He had purposely waited to write to her, although she had written several times and he had the letters with the maps and other papers next to his skin inside his vest. He did not want her coming down-river to try to stop him or to come on the trip.

He was nearing the west bank of the river now. He had travelled south purposely so that the prevailing west wind would cover his tracks. The vehicle hit the bank and he lifted his foot off the accelerator to edge it forward and up onto the hard snow. Ahead was a patch of thick bush, dotted with small pines. It looked impenetrable and a foolish place to take a snowmobile. But there was a track through it from the southern end. It had once led to a mining camp. When he reached the start of the track, Dan swung the machine north-west and began to travel along the smooth bed.

Much of this he did unconsciously. He was thinking about Sam. He wondered what she would do when she got the letter. He hoped she would not panic.

TWENTY-SEVEN

My dear Sam,
I'll be gone when you get this letter. And I know you wanted to come with me, in fact I promised to let you know when I left. But it is better for many reasons that I am leaving without you. I shall miss you very much. You have come to mean so much, especially standing by me at the trial and helping me to be myself and not some crazy imitation. There is a lot of bad influence around. I want to stay what I am, an Indian, and a Cree at that.

People like Rod and Cunard who, thank God, left today for Yellowknife are out for a quick buck. I think Cunard would like to be another Rod. He apes him. But I suppose the poor guy can't help it. He's an ugly sonofabitch and has an inferiority complex. So that Rod's companionship means a lot. But I will not talk about them any more. They are not worth the paper.

I have built a special nest for Kayuk so he can travel on the sleigh behind the snowmobile. I've made him jump in and out of it, like a baby. I think he'll get used to it, although he hasn't heard the engine start up yet. That may frighten him. If he could talk or love,

I'm sure he'd send his thoughts to you. Yes, his back legs are finally better. He'll be great friendship on the trip.

One day, when it's all over, we'll make it together. Please God, we do. As I say, I miss you very much. And I'm going to miss you a lot more. So when I get back I'll come down there to Yellowknife and visit. In the meantime, I'm sending my St Christopher medal. I got it for coming first in class when I was ten. Wear it if you want. It has helped me stay out of trouble, which I hope it will for you, especially at that Fatty's place with all those guys.

All my love. I do love you very much, dear Sam. Best wishes for Christmas. See you soon.

Dan

TWENTY-EIGHT

In among the bush the wind dropped its bite. Dan undid the flap on his parka hood and let in the air. He was sweating under the chin. By now he was about two miles north and west of the settlement and he put his foot down to come up to speed. He had to put on as many miles as he could before daybreak. After that the wind would have covered his tracks and he would be safe. No one could follow, he was sure. And no one had seen him leave.

It was quite dark in among the bush and he turned on the headlight. Long, eerie shadows fell ahead exaggerated by the light.

He travelled for four hours, the machine coming up to cruising speed and thus saving gasoline. By now he was approaching the small ridge of hills which separated the first valley from the river. It was only a rise of a few hundred feet, and it dropped sharply into a frozen wasteland stretching to the foothills. Ahead of that was a steep climb, tortuous and filled with crevasses. He'd have to take it slowly. But once over the ridge, he could coast down to the plateau stretching 120 miles which had once been a lake. They called it the Little Barrens for it was bitter, wicked and filled with unending flatness. Here met the winds from the north, west and east. It would be his greatest challenge. He was not afraid. He had to take precautions. To be more clever than the wind. To beat, to outthink it. This was the most dangerous part of the trip. After that it was only an easy run to the caves.

Dan was determined to make the edge of the first ridge before he pitched his tent for a few hours' sleep. If he were going to make the journey safely, he needed regular sleep. With the temperature now falling again to around fifty below, and with the wind-chill bringing it to eighty below, rest was as important as food. Especially when between here and his destination the temperature would drop, and the wind would surely get worse.

At the end of the bushlands, he stopped the snowmobile and gave Kayuk a run. Dan peed, watching the yellow stain sink into the snow and freeze solid before he had finished. As a boy he heard white men say that Indian pee took longer to freeze because it had anti-freeze in it.

The land ahead was a white sheet. Not a sound came from it. Cold as hell. Grey and desolate. Yet for him it held a mystery. How life started, grew and continued in such places, God only knew. There were animals all over the hundred-mile stretch of land ahead. Arctic fox, rabbit, mink, hare and at times herds of caribou. Yet you rarely saw them. Where they hid, what they ate and how they bred was mystic. The air itself, light, like on a mountain top, free of moisture, was thin. The wind always bit you. The white man was scared of it. To Dan this land was a poem to the freedom of the earth, for no society ruled it, no false gods were raised to take your mind from it. It was pure. Binamet told him, "The sane man owes his sanity to the freedom he lives by."

It was true. Dan was suddenly filled with joy. He started to run, singing his own song, a song about Kayuk and himself setting out on a great adventure. He ran in a circle around the snowmobile, shouting and singing. He tried with all his might to disturb the stillness of the land around him. But the land would not be disturbed. It was its own master.

When he was tired Dan came back to the snowmobile and Kayuk, who had been running and barking with him, lay in the snow and pushed away the top layer, licking the softer, juicier under-snow and quenching his thirst.

After a few minutes, Dan started to walk in the same circle again, and he gradually worked up to a run. He was drunk on the space. He was spaced with the freedom.

This time his joy turned to Sam. He recalled everything about her but especially her eyes. He was sure that he was in love. Light-headed with the fullness of his happiness, he returned to the snowmobile, now cold and ugly against the snowline. He ate a chocolate bar. It was too cold to taste. It had become brown wood.

Once more he started to walk in the circle, this time with a determination rather than an ecstasy. He was thinking that at last! He was on his way! The gold lay ahead. Over to the west there. Two hundred and ninety miles. Four days perhaps in this weather. The gold!

He was back again at the side of the snowmobile now. He was laughing and Kayuk was looking at him as if he had gone crazy, but the burst of the three energies that had taken him in the three circles was pent up from six months of waiting.

He put Kayuk back in his box. He sat on the machine. He inserted the key and turned. His mood fell five thousand feet into the depths. The engine didn't budge. He tried again. The starter clicked, and it clicked. The battery was dead

TWENTY-NINE

The wind came up again and with it a darkness that was impenetrable because the wind had snow in it. It was picking it up from the rocky wasteland ahead of Dan and hurling it at his back as he worked. He undid the battery cables with bare fingers. The wind curled over the backs of his hands like a razor on the skin. Under the engine cowling which he had lifted to accommodate his head, it piled in snow, soaking the air filter and the accelerator clip on the side of the carburettor. Dan cursed. But he refused to let it get him down. He said, "Blow, you rotten wind. Blow! I don't care. You cannot scare me."

With both battery leads free, Dan took out a rag from the tool box and tried to clean the insides. There was verdigris on them. He put his little finger inside the hole of the terminal and twisted to clean it. He could feel dirt coming out. He felt a fool. He had never checked the cables. For months he had planned storing food and supplies. The one thing he had not planned was a check on the battery because it had worked perfectly coming from Norman Wells.

He replaced the terminals and forced them on tight with the pliers. He made sure that the carburettor was as dry as he could and then closed the engine cover.

His fingers had little feeling in them. He worked them back and forth inside his parka pockets, stamping his feet and cursing himself. His hymn of joy had turned to a violent thing, but his determination was now set, strong and unquenchable.

He fell on his knees and put his head under the sump. It was ice-cold now. Even if the battery were better connected, he dared not risk trying to start an engine when the oil in the sump would be like thick treacle. It would take a powerhorse to move the piston.

He looked up. Kayuk was looking at the engine as if it were a living organism.

"Why don't you go and fuck off," he said. The dog put his head on one side and questioned the remark. "Go on! Get the hell out of my way."

The dog never moved. He reached out and Kayuk began to lick his hand. There was an incredible warmth in Kayuk's breath and his saliva. He let him lick the other hand. That, too, felt the warmth. He quickly returned his hands to his pockets and jangled them against the snowmobile keys and some coins.

"OK. You can stay," he shouted into the wind. The dog bounded forward thinking he was going on another of his mad dashes.

"For Christ's sake, come here. I'm going to need you to keep me warm." He caught the dog by the ears and yanked it towards him. "Sit. Be still. I've got to try to think."

He sniffed. There was no storm in the air. It smelt of an even and permanent intensity. That was lucky. It was a grey darkness still, though. And bitterly cold, the wind penetrating his parka and cutting into his legs around the thighs.

There wasn't much he could do right away. If he let the battery sit a few hours it might help. The alternative was to take his pack and to walk back fifty miles to the settlement. He hated the idea.

He took the tent off the dead snowmobile and with it a tin of dry biscuits, some more chocolate and the charcoal stove. Under that was a small compartment. The sleigh belonged to Father Binamet. He had hidden on it all sorts of compartments with surprises in them. Some of them with things from Europe of which Dan did not know the use. This time he hit a primus stove. This he knew about. The old priest had kept it filled and ready for emergencies, with a plastic bottle of methylated spirit tied to the burner, matches and a spare can of fuel. The sight brought a smile to Dan's frozen lips.

The primus stove was far better than the charcoal one. He put the charcoal stove back and drew the tarpaulin over the snowmobile and the sleigh.

Kayuk was running around excitedly, sensing that he was about to witness something important.

"Steady on, you idiot. We're going to pitch camp here. And you're coming in the tent with me."

He undid the tent bag, taking out his down sleeping-bag and tucking it under the edge of the snowmobile while he unravelled the tent. It had been Father Binamet's also. But he had given it to Dan. It had been specially made to fit the priest's giant form. No higher than an ordinary pup tent, it was made of naval canvas, not nylon. It was seven feet long and had a floor of caribou skin.

Dan threw out his sleeping-bag and crawled in with the food he had rescued. Kayuk followed. Idiot!

Dan threw Kayuk off and said, "Sit and wait. We've got to get it inside the tent like this."

He wriggled inside the bag until his top half was inside the tent, the aluminium support poles on either side of his head. He then called, "C'mon, boy." The dog bounded inside, glad to be out of the wind and sheltered by this strange blue house that Dan had built.

Once the dog was in, Dan zipped up the flap. Dan lay back. The sleeping-bag was good enough for sixty below, and with

Kayuk on his feet, it was better than that.

Dan fell into a half-sleep. He dreamed he was a caribou with the spirit of the antler-god in him and that he had to fight for his cows in the snow.

He dreamed that his rival was big, ugly and happy to kill. But that the bull was old. He knew he, too, had to kill. It was more than a matter of the cows. It was his life. But Dan could not make himself kill. His feet were stuck in the snow and his antlers with their antler-god inside them were peeling as they did in the fall. So that the old bull charged him and he could not move until the horns pushed into his face.

He woke to find Kayuk had crawled up the tent and was licking his cheek. He walloped him and sent him backwards down the tent again.

Then he slept. It was about three hours later when he woke. In most of the world the sun would have risen, but here it was still dark. The wind had dropped to a mere whistle. It was very warm in the tent. He levered himself out of the edge of the sleeping-bag and pulled on his parka and boots.

The chill in the air hit him at first. There must have been a difference of sixty degrees between the inside and the outside of the tent. It was like coming out of an igloo where you had been stripped naked to the waist.

But really it was not cold once his body got used to the difference. He prayed as he saw the snowmobile. He took the cover off both the machine and the sleigh.

He primed the old primus, clearing the jet hole with the needle carefully provided by Father Binamet. He stuck it under the sump of the snowmobile. As soon as the primus was warm enough he turned the screw to tighten the pressure, and pumped. The faithful old machine flared into a blue hot flame, giving off great heat to the sump.

Dan gave the whole process ten minutes. The bush pilots heated the engines of their planes by lighting fires underneath. Dan pulled the primus out, still hot. He put his fingers on the sump. It was nicely warm.

Praying again, he sat on the snowmobile, shifting the gear into neutral. He turned the key. The engine came to life immediately. It was one of the best sounds he had ever heard.

He let it run while he heated snow in a saucepan and made tea. He and Kayuk ate the biscuits he had kept from freezing in his sleeping-bag and within half an hour he was thankfully on his way again.

THIRTY

The engine purred. The compass on the instrument panel showed that he was travelling in a westerly direction. He checked it with the compass supplied by Manger. It was dead on. In spite of the seemingly flat surface of the wasteland, it was an uneven ride and he felt he was on a horse. Over his shoulder he could see Kayuk bouncing round in the box. He cut his speed slightly.

According to the maps he was rising. In about sixty miles he would reach the foothills and the uncharted mountain pass which snaked up through a gap about seven hundred feet above river level.

For over two hours he saw no vegetation. The bumps under him were ice formed around muskeg in the early winter. Ahead the sky met the snow in an indistinguishable line.

The air never cleared all morning. It was still quite dark and would remain so until around midday, but he dared not switch on the lights. He tested the battery twice by stopping the engine before he left the camp site earlier. Both times it had zinged with power. He was sure that it was just corroded terminals which made it fail.

Just before midday he felt the machine lift at the front and start to slow. He gave it a boost to keep the speed constant. He was climbing more steeply. He began to make out the outlines of small mountain trees. He had reached the foothills of the first range.

The wind was still very strong. When it whipped at his face it was like someone flicking a towel on the skin. He wore his wooden goggles which his cousins in Tuktoyuktuk had made for him. And he covered his face with the woollen mask from inside the parka hood. It was not the cold which unnerved him. It was the lack of visibility. The path up to the pass over the ridge was not easy to travel in clear weather, but in the greyness of the driving snow, it was very dangerous.

He was now down to walking pace and he had to turn on the lights. They showed weakly into the dim area ahead. Trees came suddenly and he had to swerve. Then a large rock, its face bared by the wind. And finally a gully. He remembered it from previous visits, and he was on the right track.

Kayuk jumped off the sleigh when he slowed for the brink of the gully. He brought the vehicle to a stop but left the engine running. If he could find a way to get the machine into the bed of the gully he could take it up the frozen stream and save himself hours of painful work picking his way through the uneven terrain along the bank. In this wooded area the snow-mobile was a hazard, but if he had brought dogs it would have been just as risky. In this part of the Arctic the dogs were leashed into a fan of caribou strings at the front of the sleigh. They were not used to travelling in tandem. They were not used to trees. They tangled themselves around them.

Kayuk was running back and forth taking up the scent. Maybe it was partridge. They were plentiful here. Dan had his rifle, but he saw no point in diverting himself at this time with a hunt. At that moment Kayuk had set up a bird over to his left. He couldn't see it for it was into the wind, but he heard the cry and the flapping of the wings. The dog came back to him proudly. The partridge was now chased into the gully.

Kayuk started down the bank towards the squeaking bird. Dan watched carefully. He was sure from the firmness of Kayuk's steps that he could use the same route for the snowmobile. He tried it first himself. His feet held and there were some places where wild berry bushes had withered under the snow so that there was soil and not just rockface for the machine to cling on to.

Leaving Kayuk in the shelter of the gully he returned up the banks to the snowmobile. The wind was picking up again. It was gusting now. That could mean that it would bring more snow or blow the sky clear. Dan didn't really care. His biggest worry was always what he had to face immediately. Simple things became mountains. Obstacles which don't even exist to people in civilisation became the most powerful influence on men in other parts. Just getting the snowmobile safely down fifty feet into the gully was a momentary total occupation for Dan. Survival meant just that fifty feet, for he could now make out in the swirling snow the jagged rocks and stunted trees that rose towards the mountain path. It would take him days to combat that. It would be more simple to portage his equipment over the pass and then, on a bright day, risk the machine. He just couldn't wait that long. He had food enough. But it was the gasoline. He could never feel sure he had enough of that.

Dan eased the machine over the edge of the gully's rim. He felt the front of the two powerful tracks fall forward and he thought, "My God, I've no more control."

The machine slid sideways through the bush. It caught the fore tracks in a tree stump and the momentum brought the rear end round so that he was sliding down backwards.

He braced himself to jump. The machine lurched to a sudden stop and careened into a rock, twisting itself out of the backwards path. Dan put his foot down on the accelerator.

Afterwards he never knew whether he did it on purpose or through the shock of the bump, but the snowmobile shot forward towards the bottom of the gully. Above the engine he could hear Kayuk bark excitedly. The scenery was a blur. All he knew was that he was in an elevator falling.

Then, only seconds later, he was travelling at full throttle across the gully bed, the sleigh behind him bouncing like a piece of driftwood.

He took his foot off. The engine was still revving. He pushed out the clutch and took it out of gear. The machine slithered to a halt. He looked behind him at the powdered sky he had created and he marvelled at his stupidity. No one in his right mind would take a heavy Yamaha machine loaded with a sleigh down a bank like that. The thought of it brought him out in a cold sweat.

After a moment he began to laugh, at first from relief. But later at himself and lastly in joy. The first part of his journey was complete. Ahead was his consuming interest. Right now that was all that mattered. To get into the caves.

He turned off the engine. He undid his parka and took out from the pouch next to his skin three rocks. The gold he had been through so much for. He fingered them. Then he put them carefully back inside the pouch.

He drove the snowmobile under the shelter of the bank face, so that it faced north. Looking over the sleigh he saw that Kayuk's box, the stove and the tent had come off on the sudden descent. He went and retrieved them. They must have fallen softly because they were not damaged. He replaced them on the sleigh and then he could not resist again taking out his rock samples and running his hands over them. He was beginning to to get the fever.

He decided to pitch camp here in the gully. The weather might clear later and he could travel easily. It was slightly warmer because the wind came across the rim of the gully and never reached him. He looked at the temperature. It was forty-seven degrees below zero. Yet he undid his parka. Above the wind howled uselessly unable to reach him.

Kayuk was trying to make him take notice. He was lifting his paw onto Dan's hand and whimpering. Dan looked down. The white form of the Arctic partridge, unmarked, lay at his feet. He picked it up. Kayuk had killed cleanly. Its neck was broken.

Dan pitched the tent, set up the charcoal stove and roasted the bird on a spit. It was the best meal he had yet had on the whole trip. Kayuk ate the bird's remains. Then the two climbed backwards into the tent. It was eight in the evening but Dan was desperately tired. He slept without remembering that he dreamed. Only hearing the whistle of the howling wind above the gully.

He slept for almost twelve hours. When he opened the tent the sky was blue, the wind had dropped to nothing. In a couple of hours the sun would appear. He liked it here in the gully. He started to sing as he dug up snow for his tea water. While it was boiling he tried the engine again. It came to life at the first touch. But he noticed that the left fore ski was bent. It was not serious. He ate breakfast and then started to repair it. With the help of the big hammer it was not a hard job, but it took him longer than he had anticipated and the sun was coming through the end of the gully when he finally finished. He put away the tools and started to pack up the tent, listening to the hum of the silence in his ears, and then he heard something else.

He could hear the engine of a plane, coming up the gully from the eastern end.

THIRTY-ONE

Dan cursed his luck as he crawled into the blue tent. It must stand out against the snow vividly. He started to smother it with snow. The plane was coming straight up the gully. He could not yet see it, but in a deep canyon like this, the walls reverberated. He realised he was acting in panic. But he could still remember the feel of the gold in the palm of his hands. He was shovelling snow onto the tent like a child shovelling sand onto a sand-castle.

His head cleared. The panic stopped. He knew what do to. He hit the overhang above his head with the shovel blade. Several hundred pounds of snow cascaded around him, obliterating the tent. He pushed Kayuk inside and crawled in himself.

He tried to figure out why the aircraft was so near. He knew it must be an enemy, for all who followed him now were enemies.

His tracks up to the first ridge of foothills were obliterated. He was sure of that. The wind had been too strong last night for them to have been there when the first light came into the east. His panic slowed to a steady beat.

Of course, it might not, after all, be an enemy. It might just be someone like Mike Hanna or Joe Barlow or even Jeff Wolgar, flying in a prospector, an oilman or a trapper.

He could see the plane now. It was no more than a fly speck in the sky. The sun was to the south of it. As it drew near it swung to the north and then back again to the south in semicircles, its wings catching the sun at each turn. It was looking for something, looking in the same fashion as a hawk or an eagle.

Dan could see it clearly now. It was not Jeff's plane. It was a big Otter. He saw the numbers under the wings. And it carried passengers.

The aircraft was not low, for just ahead the foothills rose sharply. But it was weaving from side to side almost directly overhead. the cliff overhang would hide the snowmobile. He prayed the tent was still covered.

The aircraft tilted northwards and he could see now that there were two passengers. Maybe it was his imagination. Maybe he was going nuts. But they looked like Rod and Cunard. Then Dan told himself that it couldn't be. It was Christmas Day. They were in Yellowknife.

The aircraft made one more pass across the gully and then the engine faded into the silence around. Dan lay on his back.

He waited, his head filled with several incompleted plans, for two hours until the sun disappeared over the mountains. There would be no more daylight in this winter day. He packed up the tent, ate some cold beans and moved onto the snowmobile.

The battery seemed to have completely recovered from its illness. The engine sang. The ski was working like new, and in spite of the sighting of the aircraft, Dan felt good. He looked back. There was no way of covering his tracks now. The air was clean and cloudless. He stayed to the side of the gully which rose with each half-mile until it was no more than a steep narrow path of snow-covered ice. Trees grew along its banks and when Dan had been here last summer, moss hung from them.

When the trees came to an end, Dan turned up a small dip in the land, to the north. At first the going was easy here. He was above the tree line. Dan was now a good hundred and fifty miles west of the river.

As he climbed up through the pass, he could see on either side the shadow of the mountain itself. It was very cold at this height. His feet had little feeling in them. His fingers, even so near to the engine, were throbbing with cold. His face was like parchment. If he drew a deep breath he was scared his lungs might crack.

He thanked God for the moon and its pale reflection. He could see without the headlight. As he travelled he remembered almost every turn in the pass. When he had been here last time it was with dogs, because he could not afford a snowmobile. Now his speed was slow but constant and although there was really no path or road, he could pick out small landmarks, rocks, rises in the terrain, boulders and crevasses which he recognised. He was a proud tracker from a long line of trackers and to all these visual markers he added an instinct which like Kayuk's was not yet dulled by the odours of civilisation. It told him the way home. However, Dan knew that it wasn't infallible. He had been lost several times. His uncle John from Tuktoyuktuk had wandered onto the Barrens and walked in circles until he dropped, yet he too had been a great tracker, although Dan didn't have much faith in Inuit intuition. Like nearly all Crees, Dan felt the little men were his enemies at heart.

Ever since he had come from the top of the gully and followed the path to the pass, Dan had the feeling that something was moving around him. First, he looked over his shoulder. Then, as he reached the peak in the pass and began to come down the other side to the spare tree line, he felt it again. He pulled the snowmobile into the trees and waited with

Kayuk, his hand over the animal's mouth.

But the night was asleep. He climbed aboard again and they began to descend. The Little Barrens plateau was ahead, but it was hidden by the sheer rockface of the mountain through which he had travelled.

He had only gone another half-mile when he heard it again. A noise like snow falling off a roof. Even above the engine he heard it. He stopped again. This time he was into the trees. Although the pines stood no more than a dozen feet high, they formed a thick forest. The noise came again. Kayuk, too, had his ears up. Then he realised. There were marks in the snow. Footprints and marks of something being dragged, a tree or some brushwood.

Dan was not alone in the mountains. He tracked the footprints for a quarter of a mile, Kayuk at his side. He came to a clearing. The other side of the clearing backed onto a frozen lake. Three men stood there among the trees, cutting off branches. They were carrying them to the edge of the lake. Through the trees, Dan's eyes widened. The Otter was there. They were covering it with branches to hide it. Men were unloading a snowmobile.

He could see now much better. One man was giving orders. He was an Indian. The fatter man and the pilot were placing the branches on the plane.

The Indian was Cunard. The fat man was Rod. Dan did not know the pilot.

Three rifles stood against the side of the plane.

THIRTY-TWO

For a full forty minutes Dan and the dog hardly moved. Luckily the wind was coming towards them. Cunard and Rod opened up a big Woods twelve by twelve tent and soon Kayuk's nostrils were twitching with the scent of frying bacon. They had come well prepared. Dan could see provisions enough for two weeks. He wondered why they needed the plane. It was now in a hedge of trees and the snow was already piling up against the western side. By morning it would be another mound in the rocky slopes facing the Little Barrens.

As they began to eat, Dan backed away with Kayuk, fearful that the animal might eventually be tempted to bark. He stopped his retreat on a small rise, about four hundred yards away.

He couldn't yet figure out how they knew he was in this spot. It could be one of a thousand reasons which had given him away. One was Sam. He immediately hated himself for thinking of her, but the thought stuck in his mind. Sam was the only other person who knew.

He also knew that the reason didn't matter. They were here. That was what he had to deal with. He tried to think what they might be planning. They probably watched his progress up the gully to the foothills. What action did they plan? They could kill him, but that wasn't going to help. They would never find the caves. They would save that until after they had found them. They could pretend they didn't know he existed and yet follow him until they found out. Or they could worry him until they caught him and from sheer exhaustion took the secrets from him.

Dan was amazed that he felt no fear. He had always imagined he would. He had thought himself alone in the wasteland covering thousands of square miles, and the unknown noises which had heralded the discovery that he was not alone, were frightening. Now though, once he had come across the other men, even men who threatened his life, he was no longer afraid.

He and Kayuk reached the snowmobile. It was almost completely camouflaged with snow by now. He decided against putting up the tent which would give him more warmth but leave him totally vulnerable in case they came. Instead he pulled the cover up on one side of the vehicle and rigged up a shelter so that he could lie in his sleeping-bag and keep the machine between him and Rod's group. He made Kayuk lie up against the machine so that the wind didn't blow straight at him under it. Then he lit the primus. He figured they were far enough away not to hear its hiss, but Cunard would certainly have smelt the charcoal stove if he had lit it.

He boiled some snow and made tea. He opened a can of stew, knowing it would take a long time to thaw, but he needed the time to think. Meanwhile, he fed Kayuk some lake herring and let him rest, his head on his paws and his eyes blinking up at Dan.

He was too hungry to wait for the stew and he started in on some bread and cheese. Most of his staples were in small insulated boxes. The boxes kept the goods from freezing.

Finally, when the stew was warm, he ate it from the can, cleaning his spoon in the snow. He unrolled his sleeping-bag and drew it close to the two-sided tent, with a roof. A tent from which he could roll away and be on his feet in a second.

It was forty-eight below zero when he tucked himself into the bag, pulled the hood up over his head and rolled towards Kayuk. After all, the dog could do with some shelter on this side, he was thinking. He felt himself roll up against the dog and the dog give a grumble. With one eye still able to see over the animal's back he looked out through the snowmobile into the grey blowing snow and he wondered if Rod and Cunard were asleep.

He had come to a decision. He would sleep for two hours. He had no doubt that was what the others were doing. But in two hours he would get up and start the engine. He would then start immediately to put as many miles between them as he could. They would surely hear him go. They might even follow him. But with luck he would lead them on a wild-goose chase which would carry them out onto the Little Barrens and end in nowhere. If he could lead them far enough out to the west across the desolate plateau it would be very hard for them to get back to the Otter and, then, there would really be little hope for their survival. The caves were north-west, about a hundred and fifty miles, perhaps three days away if the weather was good. If it was windy like tonight, you could add another two days on to that distance.

There was a place, about seventy miles out, where it was hard to see tracks, even minutes after they had been made. There was a marker there. He had placed it last spring and he was sure it would still be in place. He had driven the three-inch stem of a pine between two large boulders which would not be covered with snow. The pine would be leaning westwards as if he had pointed it that way. It stood at least four feet above the ground, which in that place at any time of the year was high.

After that there was nothing for nearly one hundred miles. In summer it was bogland, muskeg of the worst sort. Men, dogs and machines all sank into it like quicksand.

Dan fell into a heavy sleep, knowing that Kayuk was his sentry and he woke after two hours well refreshed. In minutes he had packed up. The wind was still coming his way and he was sure that Cunard was still asleep. He knew that Cunard would be the only one of the three to be able to tell the sound and smell of the wind. But if anything luck was coming his way now. He pushed the primus under the engine and gave it five minutes. Kayuk was already in his box. He had grown so used to jumping in when he heard the engine start that he was now preceding it.

The engine came to life at the first push of the starter. Dan slipped it into gear and started down the slope to the west.

He drove carefully, as quietly as possible, out over the treeless rocky waste, the snow blowing ahead and biting into his face, the sleigh bouncing on the surface hardened by the months of continual wind. When he had done a couple of miles, he let the engine out.

The sky blackened. This made him happy. No one could see him and no plane could take off in such weather. Within four hours he was circling round looking for the marker. He found it without much difficulty, in spite of the weather. He came upon it like an old friend and struck the end of the pine with his fist as if it had life in it.

He climbed on to it, while Kayuk barked. He looked back into the swirling clouds of grey snow. Through his goggles he could see two, maybe three, hundred yards without straining his eyes or feeling that ache which proceeds snow-blindness. But all there was to see was the snow covering up his tracks as if he had ordered it.

He was overjoyed. Kayuk bounced back to the machine and they both set off in a north-west direction. He would travel night and day in the greatest effort of his life. He would outdistance Cunard and Rod and he would stake and be on his way back before they could catch up. It was a happy morning and the sun eventually came through. There was nothing much for it to light, for Dan was surrounded by seemingly endless white, without rise or fall.

Dan was thankful for his compasses and for the sun though, because there was no way of telling where you were without them. Nature was making it more and more difficult for them to follow him.

He never even stopped for a meal that first day. He drove straight as an arrow through the last of the sunlight and into the twilight. He was hungry all right, but there just seemed no place to stop. A man needs a marker, a rock or some other familiar object to take his rest by. Dan was travelling the loneliest and most deserted place on earth. If you travelled the Sahara, Father Binamet had told him once, you could always find other creatures, ants in the sand, flies, minute specks of life. If you travelled anywhere from here to the North Pole you saw nothing. Nothing lived. If it came, as caribou herds did occasionally in the spring to those parts which were not muskeg, it left again quickly for a safer spot or it remained one day too long and the winter came, killing it.

These things did not stay in Dan's mind for long because the thought of the gold that lay now only just out of his reach began to fill his head almost continually. It couldn't be more than sixty miles to the the rim of the plateau. He expected to make it in three hours. It was then a tough, short hike during which he would have to portage his kit. It was too rocky and too rough to take the snowmobile. He would hide it.

His eyes ached as he drove now. He had been going straight for over twenty-four hours. His fingers were iced at the joints as he clutched the grips to steer. His feet had lost all feeling and that was a bad sign. But worst his head was light and his thoughts jumbled. He assured himself that it was safe now to stop. He had come nearly a hundred miles, north-west.

Dan merely cut the engine and let the machine drift to a stop in a blanket of driving snow. He covered the machine quickly and pitched the small tent to the leeward side. He needed food badly. He was much weaker than he thought. Kayuk was excited. He kept running in circles on the snow, sniffing.

"Come here and sit," Dan ordered, his brain not functioning.

But as he unloaded his sleeping-bag and placed the charcoal stove on its base, Kayuk went off into the snow. He was barking wildly enough to carry for miles. It was suddenly a frightening sensation to Dan. Not the barking, the fact that Kayuk had gone off alone. Now Dan was alone. He looked over his shoulder as if he expected to see someone coming up on him. He called quietly, carefully, as if people were around.

"For Christ's sake," Dan finally said to himself, "get something to eat. You're cracking up." He started the charcoal and was about to put on a large can of beans and bacon, when something made him realise that he must get Kayuk back first. He was scared, completely alone. The wind caught his fingers and for the first time on this trip its continual whistle across the flat table top of land brought ice to his stomach. He drew his parka tight across his forehead and pulled up his mask.

"Kayuk," he called weakly. But no sound came back to him. He called again, this time angrily, "Kayuk! Kayuk! Why the hell don't you come back, you bloody idiot," he said. He knew that if he left the snowmobile and all his kit in this wind there was a chance that he would not be able to find it again. So he walked about calling Kayuk's name with the machine always in sight. The one time he actually lost sight, he found himself panicking immediately. He ran towards where he thought it was and sure enough he was right. He put his hand on it and listened to the wind. The bloody whistle. It was eerie now. Strange, he had felt no fear until now. But he was panicking.

He stirred the beans and put the bacon on the side to stay warm. He put some snow to melt in a pot in its place. "Maybe if I have tea, I'll feel more secure."

His voice seemed to come back at him yet he knew that no such echo could ever exist in a land covering thousands of square miles without any place for sound to reverberate.

Then Kayuk barked nearby. He couldn't see him yet in the

now blinding snow, but he yelled and the dog came.

"You goddam animal," he shouted and bent over to beat the dog's arse. "I'll teach you to go crazy like that." He beat the dog again. Kayuk never yelped. Dan then felt sorry. He was taking out his fear on the animal.

Then Kayuk dropped something from his mouth and Dan realised why he hadn't made a sound. It was a leather glove. It was frozen solid and filled with ice.

Dan was groggy now. He couldn't think it through. He knew that Kayuk had found a lost glove. But his brain refused to push harder into the problem. He sat down and greedily began to eat the beans. Kayuk stood watching, but a few feet off. He threw a piece of bacon but the dog never touched it. Dan put the beans back on the stove to simmer and got up. Something was the matter. He went over and Kayuk backed away. He went further, losing sight of the snowmobile and Kayuk backed, obviously leading him.

Ten paces—he counted them for fear of losing himself in the driving snow—and he suddenly saw it. A crashed aircraft. It was buried in a drift of snow.

The tip of the right wing stuck up, the other wing was crumpled in the crash. It seemed to have been there since freeze up. The propeller was buckled and Kayuk had made tracks to the leeward side of the plane. Dan followed. He pushed away the snow. He could understand why no one had spotted the aircraft. It was completely hidden unless seen from this angle. The snow had covered it so that only from the ground and only from an approach this way could it be seen. Dan's hand went out under the snow to reach for the place where the door handle seemed to be. His hand hit something else. It was the head of a man. Dan froze for a second and then he began to brush away the snow. The man was propped under the starboard side of the aircraft against the wind and snow. He had been dead months. The skin on his cheeks, where they touched the bones, was eaten away. Not by animals. But by wind. The snow had burnt the rest of his face black, but the two grey cheek-bones protruded like chicken's breasts. The man's eyes were mercifully closed.

Dan drew back. He knew he must do something. Kayuk was barking excitedly, and digging beside the man. Dan could now see that he had a parka on and although the hood was not up, he had one glove on. The other the dog had dropped beside the snowmobile.

Dan eventually gathered enough courage to try to pry the man away from the side of the aircraft, and it took great strength. To his horror the man eventually toppled sideways and fell into the snow with his frozen body in exactly the same sitting position in which he had died as he sat beside his aircraft.

Dan covered him with snow. Then he pulled at the door handle which had revealed itself in the struggle and tried to open it. After four tries, he used his knife and the door sprang open.

The cabin was exactly as the man had left it. It too was a crumpled wreck, the radio smashed and the compass in the roof broken. There was a sandwich with a bite out of it on the passenger seat and two kitbags in behind. Also a suitcase. Dan was about to open it, but he stopped. It was none of his business.

There had obviously been another person in the aircraft. Dan wondered where the person was now. Perhaps the plane had crashed last winter and the person had tried to walk out. It was a terrifying thought. To walk out from the middle of the plateau like this would be a superhuman feat. More likely the other person walked and ended up in a circle, dying nearby.

Dan closed the door and made sure the man was covered with snow, then he bent and stroked Kayuk's neck, very glad to have companionship. He walked slowly back to his snowmobile, Kayuk leading the way for him.

He was no longer hungry. He let the food cool and he gave the rest to Kayuk. Someday next summer he would try to find the aircraft again and get the people buried. Dan didn't sleep that night. He lay in the tent listening to the wind and every time his eyes closed he would hear the sound of someone walking or strange voices in the air. He rose in the middle of the night and left the place.

THIRTY-THREE

The next day, around noon, the wind ended abruptly. It was like coming out of the water and being able to breathe again. There was no sun, but enough daylight to be able to travel without the headlight. It was at the time that Dan sighted some rises in the snow-line to the north-west of him. Within a few minutes he was threading the machine through the snow-covered rocks of the north-west end of the plateau. Ahead and up above the grey skyline were the foothills. He came in close to the rocks, like a motor boat on a lake, weaving in and out.

Last spring he had found the exact place to hide the snowmobile. Once he saw it he would know immediately. He had to do it before sunset, in half an hour. It was too dangerous to travel here with the snowmobile in darkness.

But the rock was more difficult to find than he thought. He turned on the headlight. He had cruised a couple of miles when he realised he was travelling east again.

He turned and made straight for the point from which it seemed he had come. But he reached the broken ground at another place. And just up ahead he could see the huge boulder. It was dark by now.

He swung the snowmobile in behind the rocks, felt the runners of the sleigh grind against jagged stone as they rode slowly to a small gusset in the rocks. It was half-filled with snow, but there was room for him to get in. He swung out onto the plateau again and came in like an arrow, very slowly, but straight.

He actually drove the front of the snowmobile into the soft shoulder of snow in the finger of the gusset.

He cut the engine. The world around him was at peace. Kayuk was asleep in the box. He pulled the dog out and covered up the engine. There was not enough hours of semi-darkness to make the first portage to the cave safely. Dan decided to sleep.

As it happened, by the time the sun broke through he had already taken up two loads of clothing and food to the foothills, a mile and a half west of the snowmobile to a cache one-third of the distance to the cave. He decided to leave over half of his food in the tins, strapped to the back of the sleigh and to take only necessary changes of clothing and bedding to the cave. The tools, he also divided. The heavy things like spades and saws, he would need for staking. The smaller tools, he would leave in the specially built compartments made by Father Binamet on the sleigh.

The third portage was the heaviest. It included the two stoves and his rifle.

At the top of the first grade, he wrapped each load in a plastic sheet to protect it from the snow. As he climbed, the wind started again. And he had to tie down the plastic with the heavy tools.

The cave was another three miles south, around a hill which until you reached it, seemed only to be part of the hill in front and not a separate hill. He carried the heaviest load on his back all the way up the hill to the back of the place where he knew he could climb to the cave. The last part was very steep for about two hundred feet. Then there was a ledge. He reached this without difficulty. Then he pulled himself into the mouth of the cave. He shone his flashlight. The beam travelled the walls. There were no occupants, although the stale smell of bear's urine which had overpowered him last spring was still there. He swung the pack off his back and onto the sandy floor. With the flashlight he lifted his eyes up the deeply snowed-in path up the mountain. There was no mark of any living thing. So far, so good.

By the time he had portaged the last load, he was used to the climb. He had done it six times. His legs were tired but his head was bright and confident again, in spite of the fact that he had so little sleep.

He left the final load for the morning. It was by now eight o'clock and he set up the charcoal stove to start his cooking. He had brought a small brush with him and he brushed out the frozen bear shit and other animal droppings and let them roll down the hill face into the snow.

He set up his bed. It was warmer inside the cave. He took off his parka and laid it on the bedding. He put some plastic for Kayuk to lie on.

With the tea made, he sat and drank. But afterwards he could hold himself back no longer. He left his tea, and taking the flashlight went into the back of the cave, twisted to the left and found himself face to face with a floor which sloped up to the ceiling. He ran his boot over the surface and it revealed a sheet of almost solid gold. He did it again, further up. And again. Yet again. He bent and clawed at it, watching the damp moss come away in his raw fingers and feeling the nails scraping against the metallic surface.

He stood up, rubbing his cold finger ends together to try to get the moss out. "And you, Mr Ziegel, get part of it. But tomorrow, I'll show you my gold. All my gold. Every inch of it and it's just as rich."

Dan stood there breathing the damp air and thinking. He figured it had cost Ziegel five thousand to stake him. It might cost him another five to get everything registered and legal. But he would make seven or eight million in selling it to the people who owned the Giant. As soon as Ziegel made his deal, Dan would reveal his own claims. It would bring on the biggest rush in the history of gold. Bigger than the Klondike, bigger even than in South Africa.

Later, Dan found himself taking up his cup of tea again. It was cold and he was hungry, but was too tired to cook. He ate whatever his hand came upon, feeding Kayuk fish again. And then he slept. It was the only good night's sleep he was to get for a week. And then some.

THIRTY-FOUR

It was late when Dan woke. The sun was already on the eastern rim. The night wind had whipped snow into the cave mouth. But he had been warm in his sleeping-bag. Kayuk was only visible through the small blow-hole he had made with his nostrils.

Dan laid out his tools with ritualistic finesse. The hammer, chisel, adze, compass, saw, nails, knife, pliers, spade. The tea was by now ready and he drank greedily, warming himself on the cup, still sitting up in his sleeping-bag.

After breakfast he packed up his kit and hid it on a rough ledge about seven feet up. He put the primus there too. It could not be reached by bears. He also wedged his sleeping-bag onto the ledge, and packed the tools at the bottom of the large rucksack, next to the flashlight. He then took tea, canned meat and bread and put that on top. Enough for three meals.

It was ten miles to the other cave and he had yet to rediscover it. He had marked it on the Geological Survey of Canada maps. They were at least thirty years old, but mountains didn't change. The only other time he had been in the south cave, was when he came out last spring, and he had come from another direction to it.

The last thing he did before he left was copy down the staking numbers which Ziegel had given him in the letter of agreement. Ziegel had them in blocks under his name. Once he had someone stake for him, he then applied to the Department of Mines in Ottawa, but in the meantime the block numbers gave him claim until they were duly registered by him.

Dan walked fast. The air was crisp, thin. The snow, fresh-driven. The terrain was not mountainous after he had descended to the foot of the hill where he had camped. At first he had worried about leaving his snow shoes on the snow-mobile, but the wind had crispened the surface into a sheet as thick as river ice.

Dan was buoyant. He felt it in his limbs and in his head. Life was good and he was now about to hit the high point of the excitement.

Everything was now possible. All the limitations which had been placed on him and on his family would be removed. No man could put a price on it. It was a gift of the gods. It came once in every twenty years—perhaps only to one man, and never to all men. He prayed. He laughed. He stumbled. The thoughts of it absorbed him totally. No thing, no person could enter his mind, because it was filled with his expectation.

He had the fever. The disease. He could no longer complete any thought, any emotion, so tense was his expectancy.

Now he ran mostly, Kayuk beside him. The ground began to rise again to the south-west. The sun was still there. He must get to the cave before it went down again over the rim. He started to run faster. He knew he was climbing for it was colder and there was more wind.

He reached the top of a small hill. On the other side was a valley which he recognised. It twisted south and then bent like a hairpin north again. In summer there was a small ice-cold stream in it. It was no more than a hundred feet below the hill top, and not a mile away. Its banks were pre-Cambrian rock. The slight cliff on the far side, where it made the turn, was a fault. The sort of fault geologists dream about. Millions of years ago the great mountains of the Mackenzie which lay behind it had pushed under it and in their tortuous movement, cracked the small twist in the river. The rockface split and fell, revealing all that nature had buried in it. Half-way up the cliff was another split travelling at right angles to the main fault. It made the rockface look like two loaves of bread, standing resting against each other, facing the southern sun. It was in this fault between them that Dan had come upon the cave which Jonas had told him about.

The sight of the cliff face spurred Dan on. As he reached it, the sun positioned itself just above the rim, due south of it. Dan and Kayuk ran in over pieces of fallen rock at the entrance to the fault and into the place where it narrowed to allow only himself through, and then on to the sudden opening into the large dome of the rock, which for perhaps thirty seconds was filled with sunlight.

Dan stood in awe. It was breathtaking. The cave formed a chamber which was coated with gold. And it was exactly as he had envisaged it since he last left it. His imagination had not embellished it. It even seemed bigger, more impressive.

Dan had no idea how he was going to stake here. There were no trees. He would have to bring wood, climb to the top of the cliff face and walk the statutory mile north, mile east, mile south and then the mile west, meeting up where he had started. He would have to find some way at each corner of the claim of marking the end. He had seen old prospectors scarring the rock with their names and numbers. Once they had transferred the markings to a survey map, and registered them, the claims were theirs.

Dan walked back to the slit which formed the cave mouth and put his pack sack down. He took out his adze and cut some samples. They were heavy. They were solid gold. He wondered how far back into the cliff the vein ran. There was enough gold around him to make several men rich, but in all probability the vein went back half a mile. The gold was incredibly soft and he could make marks in it with his fingernail. He took out a government claim form. You were supposed to stick them on the stamps of trees at each corner of the claim. There was nowhere to place the dull, brown piece of cardboard with the official writing on it. He held it in his hand while he took out a batch of survey maps. The first showed the area around the other cave. He placed it on the floor of the cave. Then he took out the map for the land to the south and west of that map. It was easy to find because of the river.

He could see from the unusual hairpin bend in it approximately where he was now. Taking his pencil he traced an area which he believed to be a mile square. He signed the corner of the map and dated it. He didn't think that it would have any real worth in his claim for the land, but at least the claims officer would know where it was. Later, he would come back with Sam and bring wood to stake it properly. It didn't matter now. Ziegel knew nothing of it. That was all that was important.

It was dark by the time Dan had finished and he had to pack up his things under the light of the flashlight. When he got outside the cave he felt hungry and Kayuk seemed to be asking for food, too. But he did not eat then. He wanted to push on back to the cave. The wind and the snow were behind him. He made good time.

Kayuk began growling while they were still about three hundred yards from the foot of the hill under the cave. The sky had clouded. It was very dark. The dog pulled back from Dan and started to walk round him in warning circles.

Something was the matter. Dan feared that the bears would have smelt the food and reoccupied the cave. The fresh snow gave him no hint of tracks. Kayuk was sniffing it. Something was in there. Inside the cave.

Together they climbed the hill to the cave entrance. A blinding beam of light hit Dan in the eyes. A voice said, "Come on in, Dan. We were just about to eat."

Kayuk growled menacingly.

"First you tie up that goddam wolf-dog."

Dan's hand went to Kayuk's neck fur. He didn't want the dog to get hurt. He was sure it was Rod who spoke. Then he saw Cunard's hand come out with a rope. Kayuk leaped. Cunard let the rope drop in the sand floor.

"Goddam, fuckin' wolf. I'll shoot it," he yelled.

Dan took the rope and hitched it around Kayuk's neck.

"Now, Dan," said another voice, "haul the feller in to you. One false move and you're both a goner."

As he began to move, Dan felt the rope suddenly slacken. Kayuk slipped his neck from it and he was gone in a flash. Someone fired. But Dan was sure it was too late. Kayuk never yelped. He must have got away.

The light was still in Dan's eyes and he heard, "C'mon. It's time we had a little talk."

Dan's head was swimming. His forehead burned with anger. If he could only see, he could act. The blindness confused him. Then the light went off as suddenly as it came.

As Dan's eyes focused someone turned on the hurricane-lamp. It was Rod's father, Ted Ziegel.

The sight sank into Dan's head slowly. Of course! Ziegel had his own Otter. Sam had told him.

"I told young Rod here that I'd be in at the start and at the end. And here I am. Sit down, Indian lad."

Dan saw Cunard eyeing him. His eyes went to Rod. Both were excited people. They'd obviously seen inside at the back.

Ziegel took hold of his shoulder and let his face come in close, careful not to get in the way of the rifle barrel which Cunard held. Ziegel's eyes were as hard as gold itself. And as bitter.

"That was not a wise game you tried to play at Christmas, Dan. Slipping away?"

Dan still couldn't think how they had come to be here. Surely it wasn't Sam. It couldn't be her. And Father Binamet?

It was just as impossible to think about.

Ziegel pushed back the hood of his parka and pulled back Dan's. Dan's fists went up. Ziegel hit him hard on the chest. He felt the strength in the older man.

"I said sit down, Indian lad."

Dan was already sitting. The blow had taken him by surprise and he had landed on his arse.

Ziegel went on, "We knew you had to cross the river and we were waiting. But we lost you after that. The man in the Mines Ministry in Ottawa said, Laird and Nahanni or Mackenzie foothills. First day we flew down to the Laird looking for you. There weren't no signs there. So we took a look in the Mackenzie foothills. And then I remembered. It must be this way. I remember your friend, old man Jonas." He paused to rub his hands together over Dan's charcoal stove on which there simmered reindeer stew. Ziegel went on, "Jonas was always talking about some stuff back here in the caves. I never paid much notice. I thought he was crazy. Just a crazy old man. But now it made sense."

Dan let his eyes wander again. Rod was swaying awkwardly on his feet. Cunard was openly drunk. Then Dan noticed the rum bottles. They had emptied three litres of the special Huson Bay 100 per cent overproof spirit.

Ziegel said, "Are you listening, Indian lad? So we zigzagged all over the area. Must admit we'd never have found you though. You never left a single track. And when I turned down that gully back there it was the last pass. We had only enough gas to get back to Fort Norman. Bet you'll never guess what gave you away? The fuckin' wolf-dog."

"Kayuk? How?" said Dan, his anger growing at the mention of Kayuk.

"It was Cunard here. He spotted it. The pee. In the snow. Dog pee is bright pink from the air. That snow fair shone with it. All up the gully. Then Cunard spotted the tent. A *blue* tent!" He laughed and put out his hand to Rod for another swig of rum which Rod handed him.

"Then we decided to fly over the hill and land on the lake on the other side. That's where you come after us and after that it was a matter of keeping your snowmobile within ear's range. At first we'd stop every mile and make sure. Soon we had your course, Indian lad. Must admit though, that marker nearly fooled me!"

Ziegel sat down opposite Dan. Dan decided that he would make a move to take on Ziegel. It was better now that they both sat eye to eye. "And now we've found you and all this," Ziegel said, "we're ready as soon as we've had some rest, we're leaving."

"Leaving?" Dan couldn't help himself. Weren't they going to stake?

"Oh, we've staked already," said Ziegel, reading his thought. "Brought our own stakes. Just in case you're interested, we staked three claims. One for each of us. All around this cave."

Ziegel tilted the rum bottle and let it flow. Dan had never seen a man drink like that. The other two were also sitting now. Cunard was looking strangely at Dan, the rifle on his knees with his right hand on the trigger. Now that they had the claims, Dan's life was cheap. It didn't matter much to him now. He had lost everything in his eyes. The shock of it all was yet to sink in though. But right now he sure as hell wasn't going to get shot by some cheap bastard like Cunard.

Ziegel turned to Rod. "Get some sleep, Cunard. Rod, you take over. You get two hours apiece."

Ziegel put the top back on the rum bottle and Rod took the rifle across his knees. Ziegel levered himself into his bedding. Cunard pulled a fancy buffalo robe over his head. Dan was left with Rod. Ziegel took one last swig. He placed the remains of the bottle against the cave side. "I told you not to fuck around in this business, lad," he said. "If you'd listened to me you'd at least have had 10 per cent and no troubles."

Ziegel turned over and seemed to fall asleep immediately. Dan faced Rod, but he knew that Cunard was only half asleep.

He was lying on his back. It was an traditional Indian trick. The air from your lungs could be expired to such an extent that your diaphragm beat monitored a light sleep without dreams, so that you could be woken instantly.

For two hours Dan faced Rod and Rod sat against the cave with a stupid weak smile on his face. He'd have liked to punch it. He hated Rod because he had some hold over Sam. Or Sam had some hold over Rod. It didn't matter, Dan would have liked to smash his fist into the belly which folded over Rod's belt.

After that time, Dan saw Cunard sit up and come over to Rod and take the rifle. Rod closed his eyes and was asleep. Cunard sat without blinking. Cunard was thinking of Sam. He had not been back to Yellowknife and now that he was being cut in on this deal, he had no intention of going back.

He was glad he had fucked Sam. It hadn't been much of a joy because she had bitten and scratched him, and he had ended up with a kick in the balls. But he was glad because he knew that Sam was in love with Dan. And he hated Dan. Dan was a Cree. Slavey Indians had been beaten by Crees through the ages as long as people could remember. Inuits pushed Slaveys south and took their women. Crees pushed Slaveys west and left them with the worst parts of the Mackenzie. The two tribes were as divided as Cree and white man. But Cunard didn't even want to be a Slavey. He wanted out of it all. He would take his money and go to Toronto. He thought no further than that. It was the limit of his imagination.

Cunard said, "You didn't hear about me?"

Dan stared at him, unflinchingly.

Cunard laughed, "I went and fucked your girl."

Dan smiled sarcastically. He didn't believe it.

"It's true, man, I fucked her the day you left. I fucked her in the café. Did she ever tell you?"

Dan said quietly, "Shut up. I'll kill you!"

"But it's true. I fucked Sam. Like this." He made an obscene gesture with his hand over his penis.

The anger surged in Dan. He leaned across while Cunard's right hand was still down and belted Cunard on the mouth with a left hook. Before he could recover he landed a right uppercut from his knees into the man's teeth. He felt the crunch of his knuckles against the yellow enamel. He'd broken at least one.

Dan lunged at the rifle. But he was too late. Ted Ziegel had it, but Dan's hand was on the barrel. It fired and the shell went past his ear.

Ziegel was hampered by having his feet in the bag. Rod was still drunkenly asleep and seemed not to hear the shot. Dan was on his feet and he threw himself on Ziegel. Ziegel brought up the butt of the rifle and it jammed into the left side of Dan's face.

Dan yanked Ziegel to his feet and the two struggled for the gun. Dan got home two left hooks to the stomach. It was the man's weakest part. Yet he held on to the gun. Dan stayed too close for him to swing the gun in his direction. He hit once, twice and a third time at Ziegel's chest. They were heavy blows and the man took them like a trained boxer. At last he felt a searing pain in his groin as the butt came up again. It just missed his balls and buried itself in the fleshy part of the upper leg. He drew back his right and brought it up from his toes with all his strength. It hit Ziegel on the jaw. Dan looked at Ziegel for a split second in amazement. The man's eyes flickered. He tottered and then he came back. Dan felt something hit him hard on the back of the neck.

When he came to, it was midday, it seemed, by the sun. His watch was missing. So was his compass. That would be Cunard. And he was still lying on the floor of the cave. To his joy he saw a familiar face coming round the cave entrance. It was ashamed. It was slinking. It was Kayuk.

Dan threw himself onto his elbows and he felt the pain for the first time. He was in bad shape.

THIRTY-FIVE

The sunlight looked warming, but it was deceptive. It was bitterly cold. Dan looked around the cave. All his tools had been taken. There was nothing left on the floor of the cave. Even the charcoal stove had gone.

He crawled to his knees. It was a good job he had been wearing his parka. Otherwise he would already be frozen dead. He looked up at the small ledge where he had placed his sleeping-bag. They had missed it! There was food up there, too. And the primus! His right shoulder was very tender and he had a bruise coming up on his left eye which had almost closed it. He reached up for the sleeping-bag. He laid it out and began to crawl in. Kayuk was in beside him now, licking his face.

"Good boy. Come on in. Here, boy. Lie here. Help keep me warm."

Dan lay down. As he eased himself into the bag he realised his parka had been ripped open. the sealskin pouch which carried his papers, including the crude mapping of his secret claim, were gone. They had taken the lot. Sam's letters, too.

If Dan had felt well, he would have felt worse about it. But he was too beaten up to realise fully that he had been robbed of both claims. For nothing was his battle with the elements, his secret planning. His future with all its hopes was in the hands of Ziegel.

He wept and Kayuk crawled in and lay on his stomach as a good Arctic dog should to help draw away the pain. During the next few hours he woke every few minutes to try to ease the pain in his face where the rifle butt had connected. It was badly bruised but there appeared to be no blood and no bone breakage. His shoulder seemed worse.

Finally, he gave up trying to sleep. The truth of his predicament was striking home fully at last. It was frustrating to lie there alone in the cave and think about it. But he knew he must face it and make some sort of decision. He doubted very much if Ziegel could decipher his map. If he could, it would take him days. And he would have to come back, discover the narrow entrance, stake and return to register the claims in Yellowknife. Even if Ziegel got back today, it would take a couple of weeks. It gave Dan time for some plan of action. But what? His feeling was that he would take his rifle and kill the man. Cunard, too.

The thought of Cunard brought back what he'd said about Sam. He knew it was all lies. It could never have happened. Sam would have told him in any case. But she hadn't. So it was all a lie. And that settled it in his mind. But the thought remained. It stuck hard in his throat. He told himself it was the hurt of it that made it stick, and there was nothing to the fact that Cunard's face had mirrored any truth

He switched his thoughts back to the fact that Ziegel had robbed him of his dream, and to what he would do to Ziegel if he were ever given the chance. There would not be much left of the man, nor of Rod, if they ever met. He had no moral qualms about killing the man. That didn't enter into it. Ziegel deserved to die. He was a criminal. He was also an enemy who had deceived him. The sweetness of his predicted revenge could even be enjoyed now, as Dan lay restlessly in his sleeping-bag.

The mind can travel and find itself in other places, Dan was sure. The joy of the revenge made his heart beat faster and his mind race through pictures of Ziegel's face as he died realising Dan's mastery. But the mind never stays away long. Dan's came back with a stab which brought him to his knees in the bag.

They had taken the rifle and his knife. If they wanted to kill him, he had no protection. Perhaps even now they were waiting outside for him to appear and he would end up like the man beside the plane, in a lone death on the frozen wastes below the cave.

Dan knew his head was light from lack of sleep, also he had not eaten for a day and a half. He reached up and took down the primus. He primed it while still in the sleeping-bag. Matches? He ran his hand along the uneven surface of the rock ledge. Maybe there were some in his pocket? Matches? Dan was hit by the most eerie feeling of all. Without matches he could not stay alive. There was no way of making warmth other than cuddling up to Kayuk. He must have left the large matchbox next to the charcoal stove.

Then he recalled that he kept some safety materials in the pocket of the sleeping-bag, and he unzipped the bag at his feet. Inside was a small pocket-knife, a spoon and a package of book matches. There was a prayer, too, on a tattered leaflet with St Christopher's picture on it. His mother must have put that inside last summer. Sam had the medal to go with it.

The primus hissed into action immediately. Good, reliable old friend. The primus and the dog. They became more than objects or possessions in his loneliness and frustration. He took down the small insulated tin of bread and other foods. Scooping up snow, which had blown even more freshly into the cave, he put some in his tin cup. Then he threw tea into it. The can of milk had frozen. He warmed it and while waiting for the tea, he ate bread and biscuits. He figured he had enough food on the ledge. Certainly enough to get him back to the snowmobile where the rest of it lay hidden. It was only a ten-mile hike. But he wondered how long it would be before he could travel down that hill. He would take his time. There was no hurry, he told himself.

He felt better after he had eaten. There was nothing he could give to Kayuk. The animal would have to wait until he got down the hill. There had been lake herring around, but they, too, had gone. He patted the dog and tried to sleep again. The wind was coming almost directly into the cave now. The wind had become his greatest enemy. It was even more of an enemy than Ziegel. His head was hot though. He tried to pull the string of the sleeping-bag hood more tightly around his chin. He was losing energy through his head. He was dizzy, too, with the pain or something. Perhaps he had caught cold during the time he lay stretched out in his parka.

He curled into a sausage-like link, around Kayuk, against the ever increasing whine of the wind and the strong tune it played on his back.

His eyelashes were frozen, the tears freezing as they dripped, like stalagmites. His nostril hairs stood out stiff inside his nose and the woollen mask over his face felt as if it were giving no more protection than netting.

But Dan knew none of this was bad. As long as his shoulder and groin would get better fast, he could live out several days here in the cave. He was lucky to be in it. He might have been left on the plateau.

He fell asleep for about half an hour. He had no real way of knowing. He woke and he had to pee. It took a superhuman effort. Mostly it was the courage to undo all that had become protectively comfortable and to stand beside the cave wall and get cold as he watched his pee freeze when it hit the floor. He got back into the bag and he fell asleep instantly.

When he woke, he ate again. He felt very badly about Kayuk.

"It's OK, boy. We'll eat in a day or two. Steady on." He gave the animal a crust of hard bread. There was a hard egg in the tin. He put his head under the bedding and ate, ashamed of the dog's eyes on him.

His life went on like this for about two more days. Each day his shoulder seemed worse when he got up, but much better after he had tried to use it.

He supposed that Ziegel had registered everything now. Somehow, lying there alone and dizzy, he didn't care too much. On second thoughts, Ziegel would surely wait for him to die before bringing anyone here. Maybe he was at the other cave? Perhaps it had all been on the radio, like when the news broke about Andy. Perhaps even Sam would understand that he wasn't lost. He was alive and very soon he would be out of here and on his way back to her. Dan knew he was delirious, and he couldn't stop the thoughts jumping about angrily in his head, half-started, half-finished and somehow always coming back to Sam's face at this point. As he tried to concentrate, one phrase kept repeating itself. Whenever a thought would not come, its place being taken by fear or frustration, emotions continually growing inside him, he would hear himself repeating, "Send a letter. Write to Sam. Send a letter. Write to Sam."

As the repetition grew, his thoughts grew less and less tidy, unfinished. And he grew to hate the phrase. It lost its meaning—if indeed it ever had any—and took on an unwanted connotation, like a constant interruption, a fly on his nose.

All through those days in the cave, the wind never stopped. It was driving him mad. Sometimes it whistled in a high-pitched hum, like an engine. At others it was swirling round the cave in a howl, trying to pull him out into the cold. His fingers were now without feeling, although he tried to exercise them under the protection of the sleeping-bag every few hours.

For hours on end, Kayuk lay at his side. He left only to lick the snow or to pee in the exact spot his master used once every day.

At the beginning of the third day, which was when the sun appeared on the rim, for the first time and the wind lessened its bite. Dan rose out of the bag and jumped around. His shoulder felt much better. Maybe it was the sight of the sun. He'd begun to believe that he might never see it again. As he jumped the bruise in his groin began to throb. That was a good sign.

He reached up into the tin. There was one slice of bread. He ate it fast. He shouldn't have done. Even though he had turned his back on the dog, it was looking at him appealingly.

"OK. So it's over. This is it. We either make it down to the snowmobile where you have enough fish for a week, or we sit here and you have nothing. Some choice!"

In pain, he packed up the primus, the empty food tin, the small pan and his mug. He rolled them inside the bedding and tied it on his back. At first the string cut mercilessly on his bad shoulder, but after a while walking around the cave, he felt better. He ran his numbed fingers along the ledge which had saved his life and found nothing had been left.

"Come on, Kayuk. But let's take it easy."

As he stepped out into the cold air, he was relieved. The sun gave long, soft shadows to the hills of snow, turning them a warm, deceptive pink. His enemy, the wind, had almost disappeared. The sky was violet and if he hadn't felt it, he would have sworn it was much warmer. But he *could* feel. It must be forty below, he thought. He began to take a bet with himself about what the thermometer on the snowmobile would say. He also began to plan the meal he would cook with the primus, the sleep he would have in the tent and the joy of the swift journey home.

It was strange, he was thinking. He still didn't realise fully what had happened. He would surely have been more angry if he had. He had even left the cave without turning back towards the sloping floor at the back, the solid sheet of gold. In truth the gold had not become less important. It had its place in the priority of his thoughts yet. But that priority had slipped because the very essentials of life, the ability to go on, to breathe, to ease hunger and pain, were so much greater in the prime state than the need to imagine the wonders of gold. Gold was, after all, only a means to an end and that end was nowhere in Dan's thoughts now.

He trudged through the crispened layer of wind-blown snow. Each step was easier than the last and he was surprised that he could keep up quite a pace.

He figured he was walking more slowly than it seemed because the sun went down before he had even reached the half-way mark. It could not have been up two hours at this time of year. He continued in the twilight, blue and ghostly. He sometimes thought he heard someone following him. At other times he was sure there were animals around. He was still delirious. Mostly from lack of food. But he knew that there could be no animals, for Kayuk never growled.

He talked to Kayuk as he walked because that way he kept himself company. He told him a story about himself as a boy when he had taken a pup he owned out into the river to swim and had ended up nearly drowning himself. He told him about the time here on the Little Barrens last year when he had to shoot a dog and eat it. He told it with tears in his eyes. He did not feel sorry about having done it, but he now connected the story to Kayuk and even to imagine such a situation with Kayuk was horrible.

He now reached the back of the big hill. It lay in total darkness. He started round the eastern end of it, working his way down always towards the great flat plateau of unfriendly snow and wind which swept ahead.

He was three hundred miles from home. But only a few hundred yards from a safe harbour beside the snowmobile. He was much happier. His wound pains seemed to have eased. His thoughts came straight and he was beginning to draw strength from his hopefulness, a strength which needed no food to nourish it. It was a strength he had not tested much yet. But he knew he had it.

Around the side of the hill he caught sight of the hump that was the snowmobile. The snow had piled itself against the western side. He cut sharply south, walking downhill. Then he saw something which curdled his blood. His eyes hit the southern side of the machine. It had been overturned and was lying on its side, the left track torn away and the sleigh it pulled piled in a crumpled heap behind it.

Dan began to run, his wounds forgotten and Kayuk yapping in stupidity beside him.

THIRTY-SIX

The machine and the sleigh both looked as if they had hit a rock and overturned in a violent accident. Ziegel had come this way when he left the cave. Dan could tell. Their tracks were covered, but by brushing away the top layer of snow with his hand, Dan discovered the marks of Ziegel's snowmobile coming in towards the sleigh. Obviously, they had hitched the sleigh to the back of their machine and pulled it on its side, then rammed it. It now rested in several pieces, supplies scattered under the snow perhaps, if not taken. The snowmobile itself was almost a total wreck. It had been hauled on its side with the rope Dan had been thrown to tie up Kayuk in the cave.

The gasoline had leaked from the spare tank and spilled out around the tracks, causing the right track to sink a foot into the snow. It looked as if it were frozen there. It was no use trying to move it anyway because the machine was far too heavy for Dan alone. The left track, to which the other machine had been hitched, was snapped.

Dan walked around the wreckage several times in the biting cold. He dug up the tent, which had been thrown clear. It was not much use as it had been badly torn, perhaps purposely cut. He picked up a piece of Kayuk's box, splintered to a sword. Beside it was a tin. He pried it open. Frozen lake herring. He chopped one free and threw it to Kayuk. He placed the box on the inside rim of the ruined track. Digging around on his knees, he discovered another food tin. It held two cans of beans, some bacon and four eggs which had remained unbroken. The insulated tin also had a chocolate bar. He stashed it all in together.

Kayuk had finished the food now and was scratching at the snow near the front of the sleigh which although still attached to the snowmobile was somehow twisted upright.

Just above the tow-bar a storage compartment was still intact. Dan walked towards it, Kayuk was now shaking a broken piece of his box in his teeth.

Dan opened the box carefully, hoping nothing would fall into the snow. It contained a spare flashlight. Thank God. They had stolen his in the cave. There was also frozen orange juice and several granola bars. It was the old priest's box of last resort.

Dan continued to search for a long time. He was unbalanced. The thought of anyone deliberately setting out to kill him, for there could be no other motive, was not mischief. Nor was it revenge. It was a planned murder.

If his body were found next spring and Ziegel's rifle had been used, Ziegel would be suspect. But an accident with the snowmobile and a man wandering away dazed to get lost and die, could not put the blame on anyone. Dan recalled the story about Lanny, who had been found headless on the Great Barrens. Ziegel was capable of planning a thing like that. He leaned across the wrecked machine and looked down at Kayuk.

"No. No more fish tonight. You goddam moron. Leave me alone. I'm trying to think."

Kayuk barked joyously at being addressed on a full stomach.

"Go on! Get out of my sight." Dan lammed out in sudden anger at the dog. The foot missed and the dog thought he was having a game and came back at Dan. He kicked again and this time Kayuk yelped and went to sulk under the snowmobile.

Sam was right. The gold was jinxed. He was finished. There was not much use going on. He reckoned he had enough food for two days. Perhaps three. But in this cold he had to eat. If he didn't eat he could not keep moving. He had to keep moving because to sleep in final weakness was to die. If he just sat beside the snowmobile long enough, maybe ten days, not using any energy, someone would come looking for him. But the chance of rescue was remote, and anyway he had no wish to sit and wait. His disposition told him to move.

His thoughts strayed again. After a moment he could not remember what he had been thinking and he began to wonder if he was not already dying but didn't know it. Then he remembered he had been saying to himself that it was useless to go on. It was better to stay and to hope that search-parties would be sent out. How would they know where to look? Well, they often found bush pilots or trappers who were lost, didn't they. Sam knew. Sam would come. But somehow he doubted if she would come in time. Yet, on the other hand, she might even be on her way now. At least the sky was clear and planes could fly. That was a piece of luck.

Dan eventually decided that he should eat. He started up the primus again and opened the beans. His stomach filled for the first time in two days and the hot tea warming him, he gained some answers to the complex maze that his thoughts had led him into.

First, the rule about staying with the wrecked equipment applied mainly to people who could be found easily by search planes. They were going from one place to another. Second, the rule applied mainly to whites. Most Indians could sense direction by the wind. Third, Dan Nelson was determined to show the world that he could catch that guy Ziegel and skin him. Scalp him. And with someone like Sam waiting for him at the end, Dan Nelson knew that he could no more stand by the useless snowmobile than stab himself with his pocket-knife, now his only weapon.

"Come here, you wolf," he yelled against the rising wind. Kayuk crept out on his belly. "And don't bloody crawl to anyone. Understand? That's an order. Understand? That's an order. Not even to me."

He suddenly bent over and rolled with the dog in the snow. Hugging him to himself, knowing that it was just the two of them now. Understanding how the dog felt and wanting to make him understand that he appreciated having him as a friend. Dan stood and smacked his gloves together. Kayuk barked.

Dan went round the other side of the snowmobile. The compass on the instrument panel was smashed. Someone had deliberately smashed it. The anger burned strong. It gave him strength. On the snow at his feet was a spanner. A big spanner. He took it and hit the instrument panel a hundred times, wasting good energy.

Then he returned to where Kayuk stood guard over the pieces he had collected from the wreckage. He unrolled his sleeping-bag and placed all the food in the pocket at the foot. He took out a spare can of kerosene from Father Binamet's secret compartment in the sleigh and filled the primus until it overflowed. He re-rolled the sleeping-bag, tied the torn tent and the primus stove to it and hitched the lot on his left shoulder. Tomorrow he would give his right a try. Today he would let it rest.

"Kayuk! Here," he yelled at the dog, who was already at his feet. "We're off. A lake herring a day. That's all you've got, baby. Stay with me and we'll make it. And when we get in, we'll eat all night and sleep for a week."

He was holding an aluminium tent pole in his right hand and using it to walk with. It didn't help in the snow, but it was a comfort to have something in his hand and at that time in his trek, he could pretend it helped.

The wind was now rising again, fast. It was a silent wind. There was nothing much in it at first, but it had a bite.

"Oh yeah?" he shouted. "You bloody wind! I'm not afraid of you. You're a thin whining bloody wind, you are watered soup. And I will beat you yet. Today you come from the east. But tomorrow you will come from the south-west again and that will be behind my back and I'll beat you. I'll take my magic stick here and beat you."

He shouted and swore at the wind until he had passed from sight and earshot of the wreckage. Then he felt better. He wept somewhat. Not profusely, but quietly, being sure the tears did not freeze on the red woollen mask. He was weeping for the joy that he was still alive and able to walk.

"Surely you understand, Kayuk," he said to himself. "I'm sure you do. Why, up there in the cave you thought you and I were both going to die. Surely you thought that. Well, now we're alive and going strong. So what is there to weep about? I ask you. You bloody dog. Bugger off, dog. Bugger off, dog," he yelled.

Then he became calm again. He was silent for about twenty minutes. Not thinking much of anything. Then he said, "Bloody dog, I'll tell you a story. Once there was a wind. It was so strong that it said to itself I can blow over those mountains there . . . are you listening, Kayuk?" He never looked at the dog, but continued to make up his story about the wind, as if in answer to the thin knife edge that was cutting his face and fingers at forty below zero. "and the wind blew at the mountain, gathering all its strength as it crossed the great plain. But the mountain never moved. It never even answered. So the east wind—like this grey pea soup wind now—started to whistle, and to hum and then to smash itself against the mountain but the mountain never moved. The wind got very angry. It withdrew and circled all its strength. It unleashed it that night. But the mountain never moved. Then the east wind joined with west wind and it called to the bitter north wind, 'Will you join me, I'm going to blow the mountain down?' And the north wind joined them. But it was much older and wiser than the west and east winds and it knew what might happen. So it merely nodded and said, 'If you want.' " Dan was singing now. The story ran into a wailing, haunting lullaby.

"And that night the three winds started to blow together. The mountain was tired of them so at the right moment, it ducked its peak. Just by ten feet. And the three winds met, almost destroying each other and in the mix-up the north wind took over and ever since has been the best and strongest wind."

Dan fell into a silence again. The story kept his mind off the fact that he was finally suffering from a delayed exposure to his almost hopeless position. His dreams were in Ziegel's hands.

But somehow he would win out. There had to be a way. With his stomach full and his body ready to accept whatever the wind would throw at him, he felt ready to take it on. Ready to take on anything which might come his way.

The sky had darkened again and he walked for some two hours. His pole now under his right arm, like a sergeant-major, he strutted ahead. The pack was light. The way ahead level. What else could he wish for? He bent and ate some snow, thinking he was lucky not to be in a desert. All he had to do was to walk straight ahead, rest and walk ahead again. He pushed himself, leaning against the driving snow and the cold.

Ten minutes later he saw the wrecked snowmobile ahead. He had walked for nearly three hours and ended up where he started.

THIRTY-SEVEN

Dan never really stopped moving when he reached the snowmobile. He brushed away at the new snow to find his tracks and then he found the tracks he had made coming from the cave. It was easy enough for him. To his sensitive hands each snowflake was a separate entity, and even with senses as bloodlessly cold as his, he could find tracks. He cursed himself for a fool. But he had no intention of wallowing in his foolishness. He must press on.

Next, he stood up and faced the wind. It was now blowing from the south-west as he had predicted it would. He shook his fist at it and stood so that each nostril seemed to draw as much wind as the other. To check his bearings he looked down at Kayuk. By instinct Kayuk was also facing dead into the wind.

From now on he would travel north-east across the plateau and in sixty miles he would hit the other side, the first foothills. Then he would go south.

He started out at that moment. His enemy, the wind, had

been fooled, he said to himself. It was directly behind him now. His steps came easy. His speed was good.

Again he walked for more than two hours. He had no means of knowing exactly, of course, as Cunard had taken his watch. But he knew that he was getting further out into the middle of the treacherous plateau. The power of the wind seemed to increase with every yard he took. And it got colder. There was nothing to stop it getting colder. It was a flat sweep of featureless snow for over a hundred miles.

When he grew tired from walking, he stopped and pitched the blue tent, its side ripped loose and bottom torn out. But it wouldn't stay up and his whole body began to ache with the cold, the dull, throbbing continual ache of the marrow itself jelling.

He summoned what energy was left in him and, with his pocket-knife, dug into the snow, taking out blocks about nine inches high and a foot long. He placed them around the perimeter of the propped-up tent, rubbing each block edge with the knife blade to melt it and make it stick to the next. Once he had completed an oval, one snow-brick in height, he dug again compressing and rubbing furiously at the sides. Soon he had a wall eighteen inches in height. It surrounded a trench into which he placed the tent. The whole operation didn't take him more than forty minutes. It was a poor substitute for an igloo, but it was made after the same pattern. The Inuit people to the north-east could make an overnight igloo in ten minutes.

Dan had left a gap at the eastern end of the wall. He pushed Kayuk inside the tent, slid himself in on top of the sleeping-bag and lit the primus in the sheltered gap. Its warmth saved his life. He made tea and ate another can of beans. He was still very hungry and he was tempted to eat more, but he fought with his weakness and won.

But no sooner had he won than a new enemy appeared. Fatigue. The cold was deceptive in its attacks. It didn't actually freeze your blood. It made you so tired that you no longer had the will to move and thus died. Dan wished to lie there and to sleep until he was tired no more. His body told him it was the answer. His spirit told him to forget what the body was saying. He dozed for just long enough to get his strength back. His legs were in good shape. He must have walked twenty miles. And this time he knew it was in a straight line. The wind hadn't varied. And it wouldn't vary until the sun appeared again. For the sun meant a clear sky, and a clear sky meant a wind change.

Although he knew he should start to move after lying in the warmth of the igloo, Dan's eyes were still heavy and it was an overwhelming thing to even stretch up his hand and start to unzip the sleeping-bag. But he did it. And old sores, old wounds, old weaknesses—for all disease was weakness to Dan—lost their nagging demands for attention and in the strength of his will appeared to leave him.

He packed up quickly and after he had assured himself that the west wind was directly on his back, he trudged ahead. Even though it was at his back, the wind kept rounding his face on either side and licking it with the tip of its whip-like tongue.

He tried to keep his mind on one thing at a time. He thought of Sam. He thought of her body and her hair. He thought of her in the hot spring, lying on her back, splashing her legs. He saw her wave at him and come to him to kiss him, but his thoughts kept sliding off into oblivion. He made up stories about her and then suddenly remembered Cunard and he became exceedingly sad and bitter. He started to rant and to shout. Kayuk was barking under the influence of his anger. With hardly a thought in his head he started to beat the dog again with the tent pole, stopping only when he ran off into the blinding snow.

When the dog came back Dan patted him and made friends. All that day and well into the night the wind fell against his back. Then it stopped. He pitched tent and ate the eggs and bacon. That night also, Kayuk ate the last fish. Dan had one egg left and a piece of bread. He found it hard to remember things clearly now, but he figured that he had eaten seven meals. That would mean he had been walking for three and a half days. Three and a half days, he said to himself as he sat on his bedding in the snow and finished the egg, that was long enough to take him from one end of the huge plateau to the other.

Curse the wind! Goddam wind. Goddam you and all your offspring! He could not see. And now, he felt the wind was starting again. This time it was in his face. It had changed directions. Or had he made a mistake? Dan could no longer be sure. There wasn't a mark, a twig, even a rock, from which he could tell. He could see only three feet ahead and perhaps a little further behind him. His own tracks covered up directly his foot came out of the mark.

The wind nearly beat him that night. Or was it day? It was full in his face, and very powerful. It had obviously saved its strength for this attack. It came almost level, filled with iced snow, and cutting through every garment he wore. It tore at the sides of his face where the mask met the parka hood. It tried to pinion his arms so that he could only move forward by leaning into it. It bit at his legs, making sure that each step was as short as possible.

"I curse you, wind," he whispered. "I bring the curse of all my ancestors on you. But I will not give in. You cannot beat me. I will take you and thrash the life out of you soon. But right now I will reserve all the energy I have to move forward. And I will win." He repeated these phrases until he was only hearing the rhythm of them and not the meaning. It was a rosary of hate. A liturgy of curses.

And to Dan it seemed as if the wind answered for it grew stronger and colder. It stayed that way for over three days. Dan never thought about the fact he was lost. He had perhaps known it for several days but the realisation, like the realisation that he had been beaten and robbed of his dreams, came creeping into his brain and there grew into an accepted fact, like any other realisation.

During this time Kayuk remained at his feet, taking each

step with him, occasionally waiting for him to catch up.

Kayuk was sleepy. But Dan dared not stop. He was so tired that most of the day he walked with his eyes closed. There was nothing to see anyway. The storm could not last forever. The storm will not last—the storm will not last. Again in his fatigue he kept repeating this phrase. Sleep was heavier on him than hunger. He had left the empty food tins three days ago—or was it four days? Leaving them had lightened his burden. He still had the sleeping-bag. He had left the tent. And the sleeping-bag was the next to go. He couldn't carry it any further.

On the fifth evening he found himself unable to move. He was too exhausted and too cold. His mask was a sheet of ice. He could not bend his knees.

"I've had it," he whispered without moving his frozen lips. "I must lie down and die. It is meant to be. You have won, wind. You have won."

Then he heard Sam's voice in his mind. "You must move! You must move! You must move!" Repeated like the motion of an engine.

He put one foot forward. His left. "Come on," he said, "the left did it. The right can. You do it, right."

He moved the right. Then the left again. He lifted his arms slightly to make a swing to his hips. Left, right, left, right, he repeated. He was moving!

He no longer cared about the direction. He told himself that it didn't matter which way he walked into the wind or out of it, as long as he walked.

The wind seemed to know that he was walking again, for it began to howl with rage. It was a low-pitched howl like a wolf.

By now Dan was warmed inside by the fact that he had beaten the wind and made himself walk, but he was facing a strange new loneliness. Kayuk would never make up for the lack of human experience he needed. Kayuk was only a dog. And right now only good for keeping him warm. He could not even talk to him.

Dan then realised that he was not standing. He was sitting.

He had fallen and was lying there in a sitting position, his back curved against the bedding. The primus had long since emptied itself of fuel. He took it and let it fall into the snow. The dog came in close. Useless animal. It huddled close to him, covering his stomach from the wind.

In Dan's confused, delirious mind, no thought ever came in more than a haze of consciousness. He knew that he was not asleep, but he was not sure. He tried to think of Sam, Father Binamet, his brothers and his mother. But they were all a dream he had once had. Even the gold. Perhaps that more than the rest—it was all like a book. His life passed his eyes, but he never saw it. He fell asleep, or so it seemed.

Then one thought came to him. He had been hiding it for two days. There *was* a way to live. A sure way to get the energy to go on. He had to kill the dog and to eat it. Perhaps he did not have the strength. Perhaps it was too late. He fumbled in his right pocket for the knife. Its cold steel was very hard in his pulpy fingers. The dog's muzzle was pressing against his mouth. The heat of its body melted the ice on his lips. He moved the lips in words, although no words came out. He meant to say, "Kayuk."

He raised the knife. He knew he had to strike. The dog moved nearer as if he knew, too, and was making it easy. Dan closed his eyes. How could he? He could because it meant life. He had killed men. He had killed and eaten dog before. It was the answer. He was beaten. Curse the wind. Curse mankind and its greed. Curse the very heavens under which he was dying. Curse himself.

Dan built up his strength and caught the dog under the chin, its head held against his face and its neck bared to the raised knife.

"God give me courage. Give me strength to act fast." He gripped the blade. He drew a breath and brought his arm down fast. Dan felt his arm slip. The knife fell into the snow. His hand fell on the dog's neck and he buried it in the fur as hard as if he had actually struck to kill. He couldn't do it. He couldn't kill Kayuk. He tried to cry but there were no tears. No laughter either. The dog's ears were down and its tail held under itself in a shame that Dan would never forget. He hugged the animal to him. But the animal knew his thoughts. It understood. Kayuk licked the hole in the snow through which the knife had disappeared.

"Oh, my God," said Dan, "my final enemy has won. Nature itself. Too weak in me. Too strong around me. More powerful than man, more enduring."

And he lay back, the dog on his knees and gave up the ghost to die.

It must have been an hour later that he realised the sun was up and peering at him in a milky form like the moon over the rim. Kayuk was still on him, keeping the last of his energy in him. He sat forward. To his amazement he could see ahead about a hundred yards or more. There was a rock. Then a few pines behind it. Dan felt his heart turn over. He dragged himself to his knees. How long had it been? Nine days? Ten days? He was so weak he could not count or understand.

His nose twitched. The smell of smoke! He coughed some words and crawled painfully to his knees. Definitely smoke! He engineered one leg under him. He was standing again.

"Curse the wind!" he said, but there was no wind. He stumbled towards the smoke very slowly and almost blindly for the day was bright to his eyes which had grown accustomed to darkness. There *was* smoke ahead. Maybe a mile or two away. It had a pungent taste to it. A mixture. Not pleasant, but definitely man—smoke.

THIRTY-EIGHT

As he moved into the scent of the smoke, Dan realised he had at last crossed the great plateau. Around him was the rocky first range of foothills. One hundred miles over the top, to the east, was home.

Kayuk was smelling the fire, too. His nostrils twitching and his head high. There were rocks over which Dan stumbled, no longer cursing but smiling in his urge to reach another human being. At the top of a small rise the land swept down, through trees to a small lake, no more than a mile long. It could even have been the same lake that Dan had seen Ziegel camping on, but Dan knew he was far from that place.

At the far end, its nose buried in the snow and burning almost out of recognition, was Ziegel's plane. Dan saw the marks in the snow where it had attempted to land. It must have come in suddenly with engine trouble or icing on the wings and bellied onto the snow-packed lake top. The skid marks were like the gouging made by a boat being dragged. Dan remembered what Ziegel had said about fuel. He figured the plane could have emptied its tanks as there was no sign of a fuel explosion. The tail was in the air and burning furiously. Dan crouched, aware that someone might have survived.

"You be quiet. Don't bark. Sit. Stay," he whispered to Kayuk.

Although the plane was over a mile away, the sound carried well in this sheltered spot and Dan didn't want to take a chance.

Leaving Kayuk sitting, he began to move forward. The dog whined. He turned and threatened him. The dog stopped, licking his lips.

"Shut up, and stay!"

The sight of the plane warmed Dan. It was a horrible mess, but somehow satisfying. He was so tired and frost-bitten that he moved only with great effort. He stopped near the edge of the lake to examine the wreck. The flames were leaping up the tail now. Still there was no sign of an explosion, although the crash must have been within half an hour.

Kayuk had moved to his feet again. "Sit! Stay!" he whispered angrily.

Then Dan saw something in the wreckage move. It rolled away. He could even hear the hiss of the flaming clothing being extinguished in the snow. Dan went nearer. There seemed to be no other life. Boxes of equipment, the front end of the snowmobile, the remains of a charcoal stove and food boxes were strewn behind the plane, some as much as four hundred yards away. The plane seemed to have thrown them out while it was skidding on the runway.

The trees along the edge of the lake were poplars and Dan found support for his legs as he moved towards the wreck. He moved from branch to branch, the damn fool dog following at each step. He could see clearly now that someone had died in the crash. A man's head was hanging from what had been the co-pilot's window. It was burned so much he couldn't tell for sure, but it looked like Rod. From the position of the head, which hung low, it was as if his neck had been broken. His clothing was still afire. As Dan edged nearer he saw that it *was* Rod. The head was turned backwards, facing him, like a head on a broken doll, grotesquely smiling where the flames had roasted his lips away.

Then he saw Cunard. He was killed as he jumped from the plane before it landed. He lay a hundred feet away and not near the drag marks. He was spread out in the snow. One leg had been torn away, almost severed, and the blood still oozed on to the snow. His parka had come off and lay nearby in the branches of a poplar. His hat was in his hand. From the way he lay, Dan was sure that his back was snapped. His eyes left Cunard's body in a hurry. Ziegel, who had rolled clear away, was dragging himself on one elbow towards Dan. For a second Dan thought he had seen him among the trees. But he hadn't, he was making for something which had been thrown between them on the snow. It was Dan's rifle.

Ziegel was much nearer to it, perhaps as near as sixty feet. Dan was a good two hundred yards. But Ziegel was hurt. It seemed his left leg was broken, probably near his hip. He could only inch himself through the snow, stopping to get energy to make each move. The man had guts. Dan would give him that. He was a worthy enemy, yet Dan hated no man more. He believed he would never hate anyone as much. He recalled the deliberate planning of his murder, the cool, crisp efficiency of it all and the frustration he felt because the man had beaten him. Ziegel, despite his courage, well deserved to die. More so than Andy had. Ziegel was going to die.

Dan could not move faster than a pace at a time, so he went onto his knees and began to crawl towards the rifle. It had buried itself so that the barrel stuck out at forty-five degrees, facing towards Ziegel.

He had gone only a few yards towards it when Ziegel saw him. Ziegel's parka had been burned off and he was in a red bush shirt. There was blood on his forehead which kept getting into his eyes. By now he was hurrying, and only twenty feet away. Dan threw himself forward. He began to hop like a frog, Kayuk barking at his side. He reached the rifle before Ziegel. He picked it up and thumbed off the safety-catch. At first, Ziegel didn't seem to realise that he had the gun. He was still struggling to get to it.

"OK, Ziegel. It's all over," Dan said.

He waited for Ziegel to look up at him. He waited again. He saw the recognition of his situation come into Ziegel's eyes. Then he pulled the trigger. For a split second Ziegel continued to look at Dan, then he fell forward, blood flooding the snow. He was dead. Shot through the heart. Dan turned the body. On Ziegel's wrist were two watches. One was his. He undid the strap and placed it on his own wrist. Inside the bloody shirt was his sealskin package with the papers in it, and Sam's precious letters. Dan's numb fingers undid the fastener on his parka and pushed the package into his inside pocket.

Kayuk was still, then he moved and sniffed Ziegel also making sure he was dead. Dan then rummaged in Ziegel's pockets for the papers and maps the man had made, making the stakings at the first cave. He put them also inside his shirt. Kayuk finished his sniffing. Ted Ziegel was dead.

Dan used the rifle as a crutch and moved in close to the burning plane. The warmth numbed him. He knew it must be done slowly. He put his hands inside his mitts and lay in the snow. Kayuk licked his face. The warmth began to bring feeling back to his limbs. He found himself weeping from relief.

He fell asleep. When he woke it was very dark. The weather had come in again, but the wreckage of the plane still glowed. He realised what had made him wake from his sleep. It was the sound of another plane overhead. The aircraft was well above the weather which was probably only blanketing the mountain. He never realised it might be a search plane out on patrol looking for him.

It was good to be warmer. But every bone ached with the still frozen marrow. It would take weeks to bring everything back to normal. He'd always suffer the frost-bite in his toes.

Skirting Ziegel's body, Dan walked to one of the food containers and picked it up. It held a loaf and a can of salmon. Both were frozen hard. But he could gnaw on the bread. He even managed to tear off a piece for Kayuk. They both sat under what had been the wing of the plane and ate slowly. When he thought he had enough, Dan put the rest back in the tin near the wing to thaw.

He felt better. He went over to Ziegel's body. The blood was now frozen. The expression on his face was just as it had been when he died. Dan took up his hands. He pulled off the mitts. There was still warmth in the hands, just as there had been with Andy. He rubbed the dead hands for a few seconds and then went back to the plane. Later, he was very sick, vomiting up blood as well as the bread.

He slept for another couple of hours. During his sleep he thought he heard another plane go over. But he was too tired to open his eyes. When he woke he ate some more bread, gave some to Kayuk and started on his way. One hundred miles. Once he was over the pass and down on the plain, the going would be easy.

He surprised himself by the energy he found to start into the long, cold walk. Several times during his painful passage up the side of the pass into the mountain, he felt as he could go no further, even though he had been through much worse. He spurred himself on. Sam was in his thoughts a lot. He knew now that he would be able to stake at least the south cave for himself. But he was not thinking of the gold. He was thinking of the freshly made bread in Sam's café, of the silver water on the lake that night when they were out in the boat. His mind was becoming clearer. Eventually each thought was discernible. He saw brightly. He heard Sam's voice, too, and her laughter at the hot spring. Dan became very happy again. His loneliness had gone, his pains were easily borne. And he had beaten the wind. Bugger the wind. Bugger the cold which the wind brought. He felt the wind now again, but it was beaten.

And the wind knew. It could not kill him. He was going home.

By the time he reached the bottom of the gully where he had tried to hide from the plane, he was exhausted and he curled in the shelter of the cliff in the very same spot. He had only Kayuk for warmth, but he had food. When he woke he tore open the can of salmon, banging it against the face of the rock. It was very good and his stomach never turned on it. He started out with Kayuk at his heels. Seventy miles. In other times he could have walked it in two days. It was to take him four days, without stopping. There was no shelter. He had no food. If he slept he would die.

Afterwards he did not remember much of that walk. It was a great battle with his enemy, but it was true it had been beaten. It no longer made him angry or afraid.

He sang as he walked. It was without tune and without rhythm. It was the humming of the motor of his soul, knowing that with every step he was getting nearer to the settlement.

Several times he heard more planes. It still never occurred to him that they might be looking for him. He could not think easily. He didn't even remember how long he had been walking. It seemed like a lifetime. He was always fighting sleep.

Just as he reached the point when he felt once more the overwhelming urge to lie down, his head went out into the dark, for it had been totally dark ever since he left the aircraft—and it hit something. It was a stunted pine.

He had reached the forest at the edge of the river. He was now either five miles from home or two miles, according to what part of the forest he had come upon. He soon knew. The trees grew very close for the Arctic. He had not taken this route with the snowmobile on the way out. He'd chosen the southern route with the old mining road in it. He was within two miles of home!

Then his foot hit something under the snow and he fell. He was too weak to get up. But he tried. He slipped again. This time he hit his head on a rock and went out.

THIRTY-NINE

Sam, who had come down from the north as soon as she had heard the news in Dan's letter about his leaving, had fed the three teams who had been out looking for Dan and for Ziegel. Both parties had been officially lost for thirteen days now. The Air Force rescue team had worked night and day in a systematic search starting with the area which Dan's crude map had indicated. They had not even seen a trace. The RCMP and the bush pilots like Charlie Ritter had taken turns. Father Binamet had been out in the snowmobile, but the old priest knew that it was hopeless. However, he never gave up hope. He knew Dan had courage, but he also knew he had the ways of the Arctic, because the priest had instilled them into the elder brothers from David's age.

As much as he tried to impart this confidence to Sam, he also knew that she was beginning to give up inside. He could read the girl's face and he felt the deepest compassion, for the look was that of a wife of many years becoming aware of the approaching death of her husband.

The people of the settlement had mostly been very good to Sam. But, as always, they were divided. All Indian settlements seem to survive on this division. One half saying it was Dan Nelson's own fault and that he'd always been a headstrong boy, thinking above his simple station. Ambition would have got him one way or another. And the other half of the settlement was offering help and encouragement. David, who had begged to go out with the rescue crews, suffered more than Sam, for there was little a crippled boy could do, other than wait.

It was late Friday when Sam left the Bay with the meat she had bought for Dan's mother's supper. Manger had cut off the free food some weeks ago, and Sam had been staying with Dan's mother to help her through the waiting.

The Air Force would be packing up and leaving at the beginning of the next week. The better weather was not coming soon.

Sam paused at the back door of the cabin. She thought for a second of her cousin Sherry whom she had left in charge of the café in Yellowknife. She hoped she was not having trouble. If the waiting went on much longer, Sam would prefer, she thought, to wait in Yellowknife. Too many of Dan's things were around this settlement to be able to bear bad news in it.

She leant forward to open the latch. Kayuk was lying on the step. She was sure it was Kayuk, although the dog was hardly recognisable. He was smaller, thin, mangy, and his paws were bleeding. He was very weak but raised his head, summoning energy.

"Kayuk!" She dropped the meat and put her arms around the animal. "Kayuk, where is he? Where's Dan?"

Kayuk managed to sweep at Sam with his tail.

"Kayuk. Where is Dan?"

Why was Kayuk here alone? She went inside the cabin, hoping to find Dan had arrived already but no one except his mother was there. She slammed the door again and Kayuk was now on his feet. He was standing at the corner of the cabin with his head cocked on one side. She wondered at his strength.

Sam picked up the meat and tore a strip off. The dog swallowed it hurriedly. She gave him another piece. He ate and backed away, leading her to the river.

She was crying now. She was sure it was bad news. She wrapped her parka tightly to her and began to follow the dog.

The dog led her across the river into the swirling mists of snow. Every few paces he would stop, sniff and carry on. Twice she gave him meat. At last they reached the other bank. He climbed up ahead of her and waited for her to reach the top.

Kayuk led her among the small, thick trees in that place and she began to hurry her pace to keep up with him.

The storm was making it hard to see where she was going and the place was full of rocks and pot-holes. Several times she stumbled and fell but with each step the dog was getting more excited. He was barking now, energised by the meat, she supposed, because when she saw him first she thought him near to death.

Then up ahead, not twenty feet away, she could make out a log or something in the snow. The dog was barking and trying to attract her to it hurriedly.

She ran. She bent over. She turned Dan onto his back, thinking he was dead. She hugged him to her and at last smelt him breathing.

"Dan. Oh, Dan, my Dan," she cried.

His eyes opened. "Sam, Sam, Sam, Sam," he kept repeating. She forced him to his feet, the dog barking almost continually.

Slowly, as he leaned on her shoulder, they made for the settlement. Twenty minutes later, half-way across the river, they saw the lights. Dan let out an agonisingly happy cry. "Home! Sam," he said.

She was trying to keep him on his feet. He was wobbling as if his legs were rubber.

"Oh, Sam, my girl. I beat the goddam wind," he said.

"Don't talk," she said.

"I beat the goddam wind," he repeated.

To the collection of thirty people who had quickly assembled at the noise on the bank of the river in the settlement the sight on the ice was amazing. A man was stumbling along shouting about the wind and a woman was trying to hold him up. He seemed drunk, while a dog barked as if it were crazy. And this was only Friday night. It was going to be a rough weekend.